STORY-LIVES OF
AMERICAN COMPOSERS

By the same author:

STORY-LIVES OF GREAT COMPOSERS

THEY SAW AMERICA FIRST

STORY-LIVES OF
AMERICAN
COMPOSERS

by Katherine Little Bakeless

J. B. Lippincott Company

Philadelphia and New York

COPYRIGHT, 1941, 1953, BY J. B. LIPPINCOTT COMPANY

Revised 1962
Sixth Printing

Library of Congress Catalog Card Number 59-5801

Printed in the United States of America

To

J. B.

Instruct me how to thank thee!

—*Sonnets from the Portuguese*

I hear America singing, the varied carols I hear,
Those of mechanics . . . each one singing . . .
The carpenter . . .
The mason . . .
The boatman . . .
The shoemaker . . .
The wood-cutter's song, the ploughboy's . . .
The delicious singing of the mother . . .
*Each singing what belongs to him or her and to none
    else . . .*
Singing with open mouths their strong melodious songs.

WALT WHITMAN.

CONTENTS

CONTENTS

The illustrations, from photographs,
follow page 52

FOREWORD

The choice of composers for the present volume has been a problem. There are those who are of the opinion that any composer who was not born in the United States should not be admitted to this gallery. However, in the two instances of Victor Herbert and Irving Berlin, though the one was born in Ireland and the other in Russia, it would be impossible to call the subjects anything else but American. It seemed best, therefore, to abide by Oscar Thompson's definition of an American composer in the *International Cyclopedia of Music and Musicians*. Mr. Thompson holds that "American music is music written by Americans, native-born or American by adoption. Music of the North American Indians, music of the Negroes in America, music of those Americans who have pursued their studies abroad and who continue to adhere to this or that European tradition; music by ultra-conservatives and music by all manner of extremists; music of the 'hill-billies' and music of 'Tin Pan Alley' is all American. American music partakes of everything that goes to make up America—ethnically, geographically, socially, and historically."

Since citizens of South or Central American countries can call themselves South Americans or Central Americans while citizens of the United States can hardly call themselves United States-ans, there has come into use a rather grand way of referring to a citizen of the United States as an American and letting it go at that. On the whole, it seems the best way, and in this book only the music and musicians of the United States are considered.

In the past many more composers have contributed

valuable works to America's musical record than it is possible to include here. Happily there are also many more composers working today not only creating new musical compositions, but themselves endeavoring to bring American compositions to the ears of the public. Since it is impossible to write about them all, I have included a list of books for those who wish to know who our other composers are, and what they have done or are doing. Not all the works of each composer are mentioned since complete lists are elsewhere available.

It is a pleasure to acknowledge my gratitude for help during the writing of this book, to Mrs. Edward Mac-Dowell, Mr. John Alden Carpenter, Mrs. Roy Harris, Mr. Aaron Copland, Mr. Jerome Kern, Mr. Otto Harbach, Mr. Ira Gershwin, Mr. Irving Berlin, Mr. and Mrs. Lou Paley, Mr. W. C. Handy, Mr. Ernest Oberholtzer, Mr. Philip Kerby, Miss Marion Bauer, Miss Marguerite Griffes; Mr. Richard Currier, librarian of the Harvard Club, New York; Dr. Otto Kinkeldey, Professor of Musicology and University Librarian at Cornell University; Miss Dorothy Lawton, music librarian, and Miss Mary Lee Daniels of the Circulation Department of the New York Public Library; the staff of the Library of Congress, Washington, D. C.; Mrs. Philip Bishop of the Yale Music School Library; Professor Bruce Simonds, chairman of the Department of Music, Yale University; the librarians of the Carnegie Library of Pittsburgh, Pennsylvania State Library at Harrisburg, and Harrisburg Public Library.

Mr. Abbe Niles has kindly read the chapters on Handy and the changing fashions in popular music; Miss Frances Densmore, Collaborator in the Bureau of American Ethnology, Smithsonian Institution, has graciously read the pages about the Red Men; Mr. Edward

Maisel, who has already spent some years on the study of Charles Griffes and his music for his forthcoming book, has given me generously of his time and information.   I am grateful to the Macmillan Company for allowing me to read, in galley form, W. C. Handy's autobiography, *The Father of the Blues.*

K. L. B.

Great Hill,
May, 1941.

MUSIC IN THE UNITED STATES

THE RED MAN'S MUSIC

In the green and silent valley,
By the pleasant water-courses,
Dwelt the singer Nawadaha.
Round about the Indian village
Spread the meadows and the cornfields,
And beyond them stood the forest . . .
And beside them dwelt the singer,
In the Vale of Tawasentha,
In the green and silent valley.

—LONGFELLOW
The Song of Hiawatha

One can only imagine what North America was like before the coming of the white man. However, we can surely picture it to ourselves as a broad land of magnificent forests, rolling prairies and glittering, clear streams. There were no smokestacks, no factories, and never a sound of wheels. The only dams in the streams were made by the beaver. Nestling here and there among the tall and ancient trees, along the waterways, were the camps of the red men. The whole continent belonged to the animals, birds, and Indians. It must have been a veritable Garden of Eden to the red men. And like the Garden of Eden, it was too good to last.

Though there were many, many different tribes of

[1]

Indians, there was plenty of room. They were children of Nature, wild and free. Being uncivilized and therefore devoid of the ambitions that enter into civilized people, their music was not an art music. It was what might be called a service music. Since they loved it, being natural people, they had music to serve them on every kind of occasion.

The growth of mankind and the growth of a baby into a man are not very different. The first thing a baby does which contains any element of music, is to play with a rattle or to beat it on the floor as you would beat a drum; and there, already, is the beginning of rhythm. There is rhythm in everything: the beating of our hearts, the right-foot-left-foot when we walk, the alternation of night and day, the eternal swing of the seasons. Rhythm is the first thing, therefore, which one can feel and can wish to convey to others. The Indians used rattles and drums for their rhythms. They also used flutes and whistles, and they prized their songs highly.

An Indian's music was so much a part of him, or else it was so much a part of the idea for which he wished to use it, that he could not just give it away, willy-nilly. It didn't seem quite the thing to him to sing and dance his harvest songs, for instance, when it was not the harvest time of year. Nor would he just start singing a love song unless he meant it. The Indians had faith in magic, and their love songs were used in working love charms. They held music to be beneficial, too, and the medicine men had their own special songs which

[2]

they used in healing the sick. The songs which were used in games were meant to invoke victory. They had songs and dances which they used for special ceremonies; as in the preparations for a hunt, or for going on the warpath. Mothers had lullabies for their children. Songs of magic power were received in dreams, though sometimes charm songs and healing songs were taught, to the Indians who could pay for the privilege of learning them. When an Indian returned from distant travels and visits to other tribes, the first question often asked by his own people was, "Did you learn new songs?"

As we read stories of the lives of composers it seems as if the sounds and music a man hears in childhood have much to do with the kind and quality of music he composes later. In other words, what goes in has a great deal to do with what comes out. Now the Indians heard forest sounds, and the notes and cries of birds and animals. Whether their primitive music was influenced by nature or not, their music had a wild, untamed flavor. A writer who has made a study of Indian music does not feel that there is reason to think that the sounds heard in nature influenced the form of Indian songs. Nevertheless, their melodies could never sound the same after being tampered with to make them fit the white man's rules for making music. Some American composers have tried to catch Indian melodies, and perhaps their compositions may give to a white man some slight idea of what Indian music was like, but no Indian would recognize it as his. The red man's music was a personal

[3]

and serious matter to him. It was as elusive as the man himself. It had to be free. The red man's music could no more be penned up inside a concert-hall than the red man himself could be penned up.

The First White Men Bring Religious Music from Europe

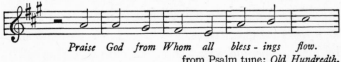

Praise God from Whom all bless - ings flow.
from Psalm tune: *Old Hundredth.*

While Indians were roaming in the wake of the great herds of buffalo, a very different story was being lived by white men across the ocean. The story of civilization itself shows a rhythm of one discontent after another. There came a day when a group of white people in search of freedom, having become discontented by the lack of it at home, landed on New England's shores.

Their little *Mayflower* sailed into a cove where the woods came down to the water's edge. After almost three months on the sea they stepped at last on a big stone, then on the ground. How good it must have felt! That stone still remains in Plymouth, Massachusetts, carefully preserved.

But what strange ground it was—so silent, with the mysterious dark woods beyond. The only sounds were the gentle lapping of the water on the shore, and the rustlings in the forest. What was in those woods?

[4]

They knew nothing of their new land. What could have made them leave their good homes in England, go to Holland, and finally cross an unknown ocean to combat the hardships and dangers which they found here?

They had ideas, that was their trouble. Ideas are what make us do things, and the Pilgrims had ideas about their religious observances that made them break away from the Church of England in their home country. There was a widespread religious upheaval going on in Europe, not only in England. It was tied up with political and social views with which the Puritans disagreed, and it affected the music of the day. Music is always affected by such things. Since we can best see the connection with music through the religious side of the trouble, we shall stick to that; and for the rest you may read history—of the years when James I was King in England, and on the continent the Thirty Years War was being waged. The times were troublous. There was religious unrest in France among the Huguenots. Protestantism was finding it hard to thrive.

When the Puritans stepped on dry land in a country where there was no one to tell them how to worship God, they had at last achieved the freedom they were after. But it was hard going—especially at first, for they were pioneers; and pioneer living means that absolutely nothing is to be had without first working for it. They had to start "from scratch."

Before they could have cabins to sleep in, they had to cut down the trees, saw the logs and clear a space. In order to have bread, they had to begin with the land itself. The beginning of bread was the clearing of a field—taking out trees, stumps and stones. After that came the ploughing of the soil and planting it for wheat. The wheat had to grow, ripen and be cut. Then it had to be separated—the wheat from the chaff—and ground into flour. After that was all done, a pioneer could begin to think of having bread. It is easy to see that a pioneer had no opportunity to make music. Moreover, when they saw what came out of the woods, they had to huddle together for protection.

Indians! People with a reddish-brown skin who dressed in the hides and furs of animals with bird feathers for adornment. Some of the Indians were friendly, but none spoke English! Others were not friendly, which made living more difficult. Yet who can blame the Indians? They were, in their turn, alarmed at seeing strange pale-faces come across the big water in a boat larger than they had ever seen before. It was natural for the Indians to regard the forests and the animals which lived therein as their own, and the strange pale-faces encroached upon their domain.

Some writers have said that the Puritans were unmusical and did not care for music. But the records are few; no one can be sure, and that is a harsh thing to say of anyone. It is more likely that they did like music, so long as it fitted with their religious ideas. As for pure entertainment music, they had no leisure for it even if they had had the inclination. Their days were full of toil at the hard job of settling a land. And, what was most important, music would have drawn the attention of the Indians. That was to be avoided. If you are ever in a great forest, alone and far from civilization, no matter how much you like music, you will find that you are silent; you listen to the sounds, and you avoid being heard by strange and unknown ears.

There was one time, however, when the Puritans sang, even though the men had to be on guard against Indians. That was when they went to church. They loved their singing enough to have brought a Psalter with them from the old country. They were very strict about their church music, and they had definitely broken away from the beautiful music of the Church of England. They did not approve of choir-singing as part of divine service. To them, that was stagey, and therefore, to be classed as entertainment, which had no place in church. In their view, the only permissible music in church was the singing of the whole congregation together in unison. They thought that a church service was no place for anything so theatrical as solo voices, trained choirs, and trained instrument players. Church singing to them was a service where all should take part, and therefore the music had to be simple enough for everybody—which meant unison singing. (This brought about musical troubles, later on, which they did not foresee.) The psalm-singing was, so far as we can tell, almost the only music which New England had for about a hundred years.

The Pilgrims had their Psalms arranged for them into meter so the congregation could more easily sing them. Their book was printed in Holland some years before they took the plunge into the unknown world.

The Pilgrim's tune, *Old Hundredth*, is about the only one of their tunes which we know and sing today. It was so named because it was their arrangement in metre of the 100th Psalm. Now it is used for the Doxology. If you will sing it over to yourself, you will notice that it has no rhythm. It is a modal psalm tune. That means that it was very old music when the Pilgrims sang it, and derived from the plain-chant of the Middle Ages, when the only music that had been written down (so that we can study it today) was done by the churchmen. The early churchmen believed that rhythm had no place in church. Rhythm to them was worldly, and their instinct was right perhaps, for when we hear sharply defined rhythm it makes us want to dance, to tap our feet, to sway our shoulders. (And if you try to imagine a Pilgrim Father doing that, you burst out laughing.)

One record which shows that the little band of psalm-singers enjoyed their music was written down by a Pilgrim. One can well imagine what a serious time it was for them, when they went on board the *Mayflower* in the Dutch sea-port city of Leyden to cross an uncharted sea, to leave all the home they knew and go to a New World unknown and from which they never expected to return. As people always do when they are

[8]

about to part, these Pilgrims gathered together with their friends; and one wrote down:

> When the ship was ready to carry us away, the brethren that stayed feasted us at our pastor's house, being large, where we refreshed ourselves, after tears, with singing of psalms, making joyful melody in our hearts as well as with the voice, there being many of the congregation very expert in music; and indeed it was the sweetest melody that ever mine ears heard.

There must have been many doubts and forebodings among the singers, as they sang to keep up their courage. How very close and personal is the language of music to the human heart—a language which pierces beyond the meaning of words.

When people who worshiped idols danced before their gods and goddesses, music was a language of instinct only. That was why the ancient churchmen distrusted rhythm, for in the Christian churches dancing is not a religious expression. If the early white men on our shores heard distant Indian drumming, it must have sounded menacing and evil to them. They had been for so long trained and accustomed to thinking of a right and wrong in music, that they forgot that rhythm is, as we have seen, a natural expression for natural people who live in tribes—just as it is for children.

Because of a scarcity of books, the phrases were "lined out" by the preacher, and after the congregation sang one phrase, they waited for him to give them the model for the next. It was very much like the way a

teacher teaches a song in school before the class has
learned to read music, when the children learn by rote
before they can learn by note.

Considering the hardships and dangers which the
first white men encountered here, it is surprising to realize that only fifteen years after the first boatload came,
they established in Massachusetts not only the first college in North America, but also set up the first printing
press. In thirty years they printed their own *Bay Psalm
Book*—words only—and fifty years afterwards they
printed the music in their psalm books. The *Bay Psalm
Book* was not only used in New England's churches, but
it also attained a wide circulation in England and Scotland.

For about a hundred years or so, the Puritan
psalmody was the only music New England had. Then
the people who came over began to bring instruments,
and as the land became more settled, people had more
time and leisure to devote to music. Thoughtless persons who do not regard history have said that America
was not musical. To say such a thing means that they
are comparing America with Europe. To know something about the history and the story of men's lives on
each of the two continents shows how silly such a remark is.

Even today in country communities there is not
much opportunity for the people to produce an art of
any kind. A farmer works from early morning until
late at night either in his fields or attending to the ani-

mals. First settlers in the United States were not only living in the country, or rural communities, but they were pioneering as well. There was no opportunity for enjoying the arts. For an art to flourish, or even to exist, it must be practiced. The early Americans had little opportunity to practice the arts. They were occupied in settling a great continent.

No country at its beginning has ever had a music full-grown. A new country has always had to import its musical culture from elsewhere, at first. Every European culture had to do the same thing except France, and her early troubadours took their musical notation from the Church. Even at the time of the great Bach, the courts in Germany were importing their music from France and Italy. It was not until after their church-music forms changed and grew out of a religious reformation there, that Germany began to develop musically. There was a time before Henry Purcell when English music was wanted in Europe.

For 150 years after the Pilgrim Fathers came, most of the people in the American colonies lived in country communities. For the next hundred years, pioneer life was spreading out into the West, so that it is only in recent times that music has even had a chance here.

Then it was natural that the music should come over from Europe with settlers. It was natural that New England should be the section where Old England's manners and music entered the New World, and where organized singing first sprang up, and whence it spread in

time to other sections of the country. A hundred and
fifty years after the landing of the Pilgrims, America
began to have her first "musical pioneers." But long
before the time of the Pilgrims, civilization and the arts
had progressed to a high point in Europe. There had
even been more than one civilization. People had been
able to live in cities and practice the arts for generations.
There had been also other influences for the growth of
music in Europe which Americans never had. These
were the influences of the Church and of the Court.

The Puritans had turned their backs on the exquisite musical services, with anthems and masses, of the
great churches and cathedrals. The other source of musical patronage—the Court—was also one which was
never to be known in America. Kings and queens were
in the habit of employing the best musicians to play and
compose for the Court. If you read about Henry Purcell's life, you will see that these two influences were his
means of livelihood and therefore certainly added to his
inspirations. Sometimes a European composer spent
most of his life, as Haydn did, under the patronage and
protection of a prince, composing for his entertainment
and glory. America has never had a court life, for the
Puritans turned their backs, also, on kings and princes.

Another great difference between America and
other countries which must be reflected in her music is
this: In England everybody was English; in Germany
everybody was German; the Frenchman lived in France
and the Italians in Italy. But who were the Americans?

They were everybody and anybody who came; the land was open to all.

America is the country where people of all nationalities have learned to live together. That is why she has been called the Great Melting-Pot. These people, bringing their music with them, intermingled with each other. The Great Combination is America. Therefore her music must be either a composite of the music of all other nations represented here, or else, as one musician has said, there will be many "musics" coming from the Melting-Pot.

As time went on, the people who settled in Pennsylvania were the music-loving Welsh, Germans and Swedes, who brought their music with them. From Bohemia, the most musical region of Europe, came a Moravian sect who settled in Bethlehem, Pennsylvania, where their influence on music has come down to our times. Every year people still go to hear the Bethlehem Bach Choir.

There may have been some music in the Virginia Colony which was settled even before the year when the Pilgrims came to New England, but the records do not give us much information. We do know, however, that it was from the psalm-singing Yankees, whose interest in music was, if not broad, at least keen, earnest and sincere, that the singing-societies and singing-schools came into existence. And it was through them that music was cultivated throughout the rest of the country.

The Puritans' music suffered at first, when part-singing sank to one part. They suffered from a lack of musical instruction and from a lack of instruments. In time, instruments were brought over from the old country, and the New Englanders brought out new song-books of their own. They knew they were having musical troubles, and realized that they must learn to read their notes.

At first, as we have seen, their *Bay Psalm Book* did not even have the music printed in it, since no one could read it. Gradually their books on the singing of psalm tunes included instruction—what they called *Grounds and Rules of Musick*. For a while, however, this confused the Puritans again, and they said, "If we once begin to sing by note, the next thing will be to pray by rule, and preach by rule," and they were afraid they would go right back again to their original discontent with having too many rules in their worship. The years went by as they fussed and worried, wanting to sing better and not knowing how. They went at it carefully, however, and in time they were able to have rules in music, to read their notes, and so learn to sing and play without letting it interfere with their Sunday-go-to-meetin'.

In the year 1770 which saw the birth of Beethoven in Germany, the earliest singing-schools were organized in New England. Their successors for a long time used no songs but those which could also be sung in the meeting-house without offense. That year the *New England Psalm-Singer* was printed in Boston. It was compiled by one of the earliest of American composers, named

William Billings. The frontispiece was engraved by a gentleman, well known today, named Paul Revere. He is not well known because he engraved the psalm-tune book, however. He is well known now because of a horseback ride he took one night—five years later.

OUR FIRST AMERICAN COMPOSERS

"My Days Have Been So Wondrous Free"

About the time we became a country, independent and free, we had a composer of our own. The first American composer was Francis Hopkinson, by birth a Philadelphian. Some years before Paul Revere had engraved the psalm-tune collection, Hopkinson composed an *Ode to Music,* and a song, *My Days Have Been So Wondrous Free.* It seems quite fitting that our first composer should have been a friend of George Washington, and one of the signers of the Declaration of Independence. Our second president, John Adams, described the composer once in a letter to his wife. He informed her that Hopkinson was:

> . . . one of your pretty, little, curious, ingenious men. His head is not bigger than a large apple. I have not met with anything in natural history more amusing and entertaining than his personal appearance, yet he is genteel and well bred, and is very social.

Another early composer was William Billings, a tanner of Boston. He was a "character." He loved

[15]

music so enthusiastically that he gave up his tanning business to make music his profession. In those days a man could not live by music in this country, and Billings died in poverty. But he became widely known in New England, and his music was played as far away as Philadelphia. His musical enthusiasm was greater than his ability to play or sing. He was handicapped by being blind in one eye, having a withered arm, legs of different length, and a harsh voice! His ears, apparently, were all right. Besides the book of psalm tunes which Paul Revere engraved, Billings wrote what he called "fuguing pieces," which he considered to be "more than twenty times as powerful as the old slow tunes." At a concert in Boston two of his anthems were sung, and the concert ended with the *Hallelujah Chorus* from *The Messiah* by Handel.

Some years after the War of the American Revolution the first orchestral score was published in the United States. It was called *The Death Song of an Indian Chief.*

OUR NATIONAL AIRS APPEAR

"*Sweet Land of Liberty,*
Of Thee I sing"

When the descendants of the people who had worked so hard and endured so much to be free, found that their freedom was threatened, they prepared to fight. When feelings run high, music is a wonderful outlet. It was natural that our national airs should be born in times like these.

The first, most popular, tune in America was not born here, however. It is characteristic of the gay, impertinent little tune of *Yankee Doodle* that it insists on being mentioned before the national airs. The tune to *Yankee Doodle* is old, and perhaps that is the reason.

When *Yankee Doodle* was sung by the British soldiers to ridicule the New England farmers, it was the same simple, rustic air which we know today. But it is supposed to have been used as a chant in the churches of Italy over a thousand years ago. In that case it was sung slowly, with the notes of the same time-value, and therefore without rhythm. If we can trust this theory the tune was, in time, carried out of church, and sung by the peasants in the vineyards of southern Europe. Words were naturally fitted to it. Gradually the tune crept north to Holland, where "yanker" was the old Dutch word for "Johnny." "Doodle" was from an old Frisian word meaning a dull fellow or "dumb-bell." As the centuries rolled by, the tune reached England where the nurse-maids sang the tune to the babies, with the words:

> Lucy Locket lost her pocket;
> Kitty Fisher found it.
> Nothing in it, nothing on it,
> But the binding round it.

Now no tune sticks closer than one we learn in the nursery. When the days of the Commonwealth arrived in England, and for a time there was no king, the Protector, Oliver Cromwell, rode to London town to become ruler. He rode from Canterbury on a Kentish pony. He wore a little round hat with a single feather, and was laughed at by the gay Cavaliers, or king's men. Their song of ridicule was,

> Yankee Doodle came to town
> Upon a Kentish pony;
> Stuck a feather in his hat
> And called him macaroni.

Macaroni was the name for the tight clothes in the Italian style, which were worn by the young men of fashion.

A hundred years after that the British red coats came to America, and began ridiculing the country farmers of New England. The simple rustics went to town to gaze with wonder upon the exquisitely uniformed British soldiers with their cannons. How green and queer these farmers looked to the traveled soldiers! The easiest thing to do, impolite as it is, is to ridicule and make fun of others. So the British troops used to gather outside the churches on Sundays while the New Englanders were singing their psalm tunes, taunting them and trying to outsing them. Their song was *Yankee Doodle*.

On the April night in 1775 when British troops marched out of Boston towards Lexington, they kept in step while singing *Yankee Doodle*. Ahead of them—though they did not know it—was a real Yankee, Paul Revere, and he was "riding on his pony." There came a day when the tables were turned, and the British General Cornwallis sadly surrendered at Yorktown. The defeated British band played, appropriately, *The World Turned Upside Down*, but it was the American band who answered (equally appropriately) with *Yankee Doodle*.

The son of the first American composer was Joseph Hopkinson, in his day the finest harpsichord player in America, and he was the author of *Hail Columbia*. He told the story of how he came to write it. It was at a time when France was giving America some trouble. The second president, John Adams, was in office. Feeling ran high again, and two political parties were taking sides. One Saturday afternoon in the summer of 1798, while Congress was sitting in Philadelphia debating its problems, a singer named Gilbert Fox called on Hopkinson, whom he had known at school.

Mr. Fox was in a quandary. On the following Monday night, he was having a benefit at the theatre. He was supposed to sing a new patriotic song to the *President's March*. The trouble, he explained to Mr. Hopkinson, was that none of the poets of the theatrical group had been able to think up the words. It was difficult to make a patriotic song that would not offend one of the parties. He wondered if Mr. Hopkinson could help him out. Mr. Hopkinson said he'd see what he could do.

The next afternoon, Sunday, the singer came again. Mr. Hopkinson said the words were ready. He had made them patriotic in sentiment, but in such a way that both parties could sing them. When Mr. Fox sang the song on Monday night, he had "great applause," and it found favor at once. Only two days later, Benjamin Carr, who had the first music store in America, advertised the song, *Hail Columbia.*

The words of our national anthem, *The Star Spangled Banner,* were written on the spur of the moment, when feeling was most intense. It was during the War of 1812, on the night of September 13, 1814.

The British had captured an American physician and were holding him captive on the fleet anchored off Baltimore. Francis Scott Key, a young lawyer, arranged to go out under a flag of truce and ask for the doctor's release. But the British were planning an attack on Fort McHenry preparatory to taking Baltimore, and they detained Key for several days until their attack should be over. Therefore Key was himself a prisoner on the night of September 13th, when he watched the beginning of the British bombardment. They had anchored the ship he was on where he could not avoid seeing the fight. The Americans had suffered losses during the previous weeks, and even their capitol in Washington had been burned by the enemy. The British were confident they could succeed in their new attack, and expected Key to witness his country's humiliation. It was a terrible night for him. He paced the decks, unable to sleep, trying to see through the dark-

ness where every shell landed on the fort. In the twi-
light he had seen a great flag of stars and stripes flying
in the breeze above the fort. Would he see that same
flag flying in the morning?

Gradually the darkness began to lift, and streaks
of light appeared in the east. There was a mist above
the water and he could not see the fort. The bombs
and firing had ceased suddenly sometime in the night.
Why? he wondered. There was no message. If only
he could see which flag was flying.

Suddenly a breeze began to blow the mists away,
and with his eyes strained, he saw what he had hardly
dared to hope for. With a corner shot away and one
star gone, the flag that was still flying above the fort
was the *Star Spangled Banner,* and he sang in his heart,
*O long may it wave o'er the land of the free and the
home of the brave.*

Mr. Key was so excited that he snatched an en-
velope out of his pocket and began writing down the
words that came to him. When he reached Baltimore,
he gave them to a printer, and the verses were struck
off on a handbill. That very night the words were sung
in a tavern in Baltimore. They were sung to an English
drinking-tune which was popular at the time. From that
moment the song became American. Why not? Americans once came from England. The words, the tune,
the times were stirring, and the song became, through
constant use, the American national anthem.

The hymn, *America,* is one of the few patriotic songs that has absolutely no reference to war. It is truly a national hymn. The words were written by Samuel Francis Smith over a hundred years ago. He, too, told how he came to write it.

There was a gentleman who had come from Europe bringing some German music-books with him. He gave these to the hymn-writer, Lowell Mason, who could read the music but not the German. Mr. Mason, in turn, handed them to Smith, a clergyman, with the request that Smith look through them and see what he could find in them that the musician, Mason, might use. Mr. Smith said:

> Accordingly, one leisure afternoon, I was looking over the books, and fell in love with the tune of *God Save the King,* and at once took up my pen and wrote the piece. . . . It was struck out at a sitting, without the slightest idea that it would ever attain the popularity it has since enjoyed. . . . The first time it was sung publicly was at a children's celebration of American independence.

As history rolls away and new stories unfold it seems rather fitting to have the American national hymn the very same tune as the English *God Save the King;* rather significant again, that the *Star Spangled Banner* is sung to an old English popular song. The adoption of the mother country's tunes seems to express a spirit of letting "bygones be bygones" and "let's pull together." Perhaps the meaning of music goes deeper than guns. Perhaps we sing what is, in effect, a handshake over the past.

The tune of *America* is not only the same as *God Save the King*, but it serves several other nations as well. The language of music indeed knows no dividing line between nations. Perhaps if all the laws were songs, the nations would all be friends.

MUSIC GROWS IN THE UNITED STATES: AMERICAN HYMNS

"Singin'-all-day-and-dinner-on-the-grounds"

This busy land of ours has been busy from the start. William Billings, the queer-looking musical enthusiast and ex-tanner of Boston town, was doing his pioneering in music about the time that Beethoven was born in far-off Germany. Besides his composition, Billings busied himself with organizing the first "Sacred Singing School." Still in existence, it is now the Stoughton Musical Society. Singing-schools began to spring up in great numbers, and were the musical pioneers of the New World.

They were very important socially because through them singing was gradually released from the authority of the church, and became an enjoyment of the people whether churchmen or not. The schools were important in developing a new profession in the country—the profession of music-teacher. They were important in creating a new commodity that could be bought and sold, and that commodity was published music. The first singing-teachers were music-salesmen, who advertised and sold the books of psalm tunes. Newspapers began to contain "ads" of singing-teachers and song collections. There were dozens of these advertisements to one of a dancing-master or of a musician eager to teach the German flute, harpsichord or violin. Instruments had already begun to be made in America, but a general proficiency in playing them was not even to begin for another hundred years, until after the railroads were built and transportation was made easier. It was not until "ragtime" music became a fad that instrument-playing spread noticeably among the people.

The first thing the singing-societies had to do was to instruct the singers in reading music. The first books of modal psalm tunes to contain music had no bar lines, no time signatures. Since the modal music lacked rhythm, bar lines and time signatures were not felt to be necessary. The British redcoats who hung around the New England churches may have heard singing that struck them as being pretty "green." One can imagine how difficult it was for a congregation to begin a hymn, when there was no instrument and no knowledgeable singer to start them off. The earnest voices must have felt around, pathetically, for a common pitch, and struggled to begin and end their phrases together. The singers had to guess at the intervals. The sharpings and the flattings must have been on the same basis as the idea of the marching soldier-boy who thought, "they're all out of step but me." Yet the seriousness and earnestness gave dignity to the undertaking.

In Europe, hundreds of years before, a system of note-singing had been developed which is still known and used in schools today. Syllables were given to the notes. Every one has sung his *do re mi*. In one section of England, however, the *do re mi* had simmered down to *fa sol la* (with a *mi* thrown in), and these syllables were sung in Shakespeare's time when Elizabeth was Queen.

When the singing-schools sprang up, there was a need for printed music and better instruction in the "grounds"—or rules, so that the "scholers" could have their books with "helps-to-read," as well as "an abundance of attractive music for practice and social enjoyment." To simplify learning to sing from a book, shapes were given to the notes, so that a pupil could tell at a glance whether the note was a *sol* or a *fa*. Then the Doxology looked like this:

OLD 100

Cheerful

The *Old Hundredth* Psalm Tune was singled out as a model tune "for Psalms of praise and cheerfulness."

On the staff, in the oldest known shape-note book, called *The Easy Instructor*, the tune looked like this:

Sharp Key on A

The major keys were called sharp keys and the minor were called flat keys. It wasn't a very clear way of naming the modes, because when it came to C major, they called it sharp key in C, although that key has no sharps.

Since the singing-schools were "music's declaration of independence," they usually met in a tavern. Music was spreading out of church. The singers brought their own candles, which they stood with their books on benches. Sitting in a semi-circle two or three rows deep, they spent three-hour sessions for twenty-four afternoons or evenings in learning their clefs, note-values, and all the things boys and girls learn now before they ever grow up. The great object was the "exhibition" held in the meeting-house at the end of the course, when the class could show what it had learned. Then the itinerant singing-school teacher went on to another village or locality, organized another class for twenty-four lessons, and peddled the books of song collections. The songs for these schools and societies gradually became more elaborate and lengthy than the plain and easy tunes that were used in church.

When organs came to the churches of the eastern cities the singing-school master was no longer needed. Better music and musicians came from Europe along with the imported instruments, and America began to have factories where she made her own. The "shape-noters" were pushed—like the frontier—farther west and south. Better educational systems were also introduced from Europe together with the *do re mi.* The "fasola" teachers (as they were called) had to go where the people still knew nothing better. In this way the shape-note system developed an influence for separating country music from city music; and folk-singing from art-singing. In the South, the cities and the communities along the coast had more advanced music. Visiting artists from Europe gave concerts. It was a region of big planters and slave-owners. The country gentlemen, George Washington included, enjoyed dancing their minuets, and there seems to have been a certain graciousness in their ways of living. But back in the hills and mountain country, in the regions which were difficult to find, when once the fasola music entered, it stuck. In these regions it may still be possible to come across fasola singers, whose shape notation was called "buckwheat notes." Very recently, at least, there have been conventions of fasola singers. The town where the convention met would be full of people who had come from miles around. The "teacher" would have nothing to aid him but a tuning-fork. In the land of the white spirituals, there would be a "singin'-all-day-and-dinner-on-the-grounds."

But with radios and victrolas spreading a newer music, it is doubtful whether such "singin's" will be in existence much longer. The old country-style is likely to recede until it disappears entirely. The pioneer and pioneer music are of the past. Already the old people do not find the "singin' " the way it was in their youth, and they wag their heads and say,

> So music past is obsolete,
> And yet 'twas sweet, 'twas passing sweet.

While the "buckweat notes" were being taught ever farther and farther inland in the rural districts, musicians had grown up in our Eastern cities, and the colleges developed our own composers. Considering the kind of music first practiced in America it was natural that the first American composers should have been hymn-writers. Lowell Mason, a friend of the writer of the words of *My Country 'tis of Thee,* was the author of many dignified hymns, such as *Nearer My God to Thee* and *My Faith Looks up to Thee,* which we use today.

It was about this time that American hymnody branched off into two different types. The better type were stately hymns like those of Mason; but another kind, known as the gospel hymns, began to appear. These were used chiefly in camp-meetings, revivalist campaigns, and in some of the Sunday Schools. Because their purpose was to arouse emotion to a high pitch, they were more personal and sentimental. During the period of the hymn revival, rhythmic effects began to be appreciated and liked for their own sake. The country was growing fast; inventions were discovered; railways were laid; people were thinking of music as a source of pleasure and enjoyment. Sentimentality came into fashion. In the parlors, after supper, the pianos would be opened and the family would gather round to sing sentimental ballads. It was merely keeping in step with the times that sentimental hymns also appeared. When the sentiment was sincere and simple, the hymns had a chance of lasting. Sometimes, however, this type of hymn was written by a "musician" who did not know how to write a melody to fit the words.

But many of the evangelical hymns and sentimental songs have not been forgotten. It was the Gospel hymn which our Southern Negroes heard from the white preachers, hymns such as *Shall We Gather at the River?* and *Will There Be Any Stars in My Crown?* and *When the Roll is Called up Yonder I'll be There.*

PEOPLE FROM AFRICA CREATE NEGRO SPIRITUALS

"Swing low, sweet chariot,
Comin' fo' to carry me Home."

The year before the *Mayflower* landed her earnest little band of psalm-singers on New England's rocky shores, the first slave-ship from Africa drew up along the Southern coast. The white settlers had begun to import Negro men as slaves. How ironic, that in a country where the white men came to be free, the black men came enslaved! However, unlike the whites, they were totally uneducated, fresh from the jungle and tribal life. Civilization requires time. They had first to learn the white man's language, then they learned to work for him. Unlike the red men, the disposition of the Negroes was conformable. They were easy-going, sweet of voice and nature, inclined to both sad and happy moods. They could adjust themselves to living with the whites. The Indians, reserved and aloof, could not submit to slavery. They preferred to die—free.

People of the Negro race have a deep instinct for

[30]

rhythm and song. In their native Africa, they had their dances and their drums. They brought with them what they remembered, for they had no system of writing music and consequently no books. Their music was elementary and tribal.

The greatest thing about the Negro is that he is completely unhindered by any feeling of restraint, and no matter what his mood, whether gay or sad, whether singing or dancing, he can put himself heart and soul into his music. In other words, he can "give."

From the white preachers, the colored folk learned about the white man's religion, and with it they heard the gospel songs. It was the gospel song which appealed most to the Negro, and which he interpreted into a different music. Some of the white composers wrote songs which were cheap and tawdry by being over-sentimental and obvious. The Negroes did not write songs, they didn't know enough. They could not read, and they could not write. But they could feel. Their songs were not composed, they just "came." Their greatest quality was simplicity and sincerity. From the slaves came heartfelt cries—cries in song, pure and simple. Some writers have said that the Negroes in their spirituals improved on the white man's gospel songs. Instead of singing *Shall We Gather at the River, the Beautiful, the Beautiful River?*, the Negro sang simply *Roll, Jordan, Roll*. Instead of singing a self-conscious *When the Roll is Called up Yonder I'll be There*, the Negro cried,

I Want to be Ready, and *Dese Bones Gwine to Rise Again,* or *On that Great Gittin'-up Mornin'.*

In time the Negroes were taught by white preachers, and the colored people had their own Sabbath meetings and their own colored preachers. A white lady who attended a Negro service in the South wrote down her description of it. When she entered the "little ramshackle meeting-house" the Negroes had assembled, dressed in their best Sunday-go-to-meetin' clothes. The

> service had already begun before we came and the congregation, silent and devout, sat in rows on the rough backless benches. The preacher now exhorted his flock to prayer, and the people with one movement surged forward from the benches and down onto their knees, every black head deep-bowed in an abandonment of devotion. Then the preacher began in a quavering voice a long supplication. Here and there came an uncontrollable cough from some kneeling penitent or the sudden squall of a restless child; and now and again an ejaculation, warm with entreaty, "O Lord!" or a muttered "Amen, Amen"—all against the background of the praying, endless praying.
>
> Minutes passed, long minutes of strange intensity. The mutterings, the ejaculations grew louder, more dramatic, till suddenly I felt the creative thrill dart through the people like an electric vibration, that same half-audible hum arose—emotion was gathering atmospherically, as clouds gather—and then, up from the depths of some "sinner's" remorse and imploring, came a pitiful little plea, a real Negro "moan," sobbed in musical

cadence. From somewhere in that bowed gathering another voice improvised a response; the plea sounded again, louder this time and more impassioned; then other voices joined in the answer, shaping it into a musical phrase; and so, before our ears, as one might say, from this molten metal of music a new song was smithied out, composed then and there by no one in particular and by everyone in general.

The Negro "spiritual" came into existence. The simple black men transferred the Bible stories into their own experiences.

In tribal ceremonies in Africa, the men and women could work themselves into frenzies of mood, religious or warlike—whatever their aim—by their drumming, droning and singing. In the United States, they could work themselves into frenzies of happiness or ecstasy in their church meetings. They would push back the church benches and tramp for hours in a line, round and round the church room, singing and swaying to their slow, shuffling walk. Their singing was, as usual with them, made up as they went along. They might have taken a line from the Bible as read by the preacher, and made up their whole song upon it, with much repetition and with slight changes contributed by different individuals. These services were called "shoutin' meetings." As a young boy, Stephen Foster was permitted to attend sometimes, a "shoutin' " Negro church.

The Negroes had songs also that were not religious. They had their work songs for cotton-picking, corn-shucking, steamboat songs, railroad songs of the section gangs. For any situation or experience, these music-loving people could make a song. They had their music for pure entertainment as well.

Many of their spirituals and secular songs had their verses started by a leader, and the crowd would sing the rest. For instance, the leader would sing;

I got a robe, you got a robe;

and everybody sang:

All God's chillun got a robe,
When I get to heab'm, gonna put on my robe,
Gonna shout all over God's heab'm!

ENTERTAINMENT MUSIC: THE MINSTREL SHOWS

*"Turn about, an' wheel about
An' do jis so,
An' ebery time I turn about
I jump Jim Crow."*

As the American cities grew both in number and in size, music became more and more of a business. The country grew wealthy, and foreign musicians and artists came over to sell their wares for American money. Concerts were given and symphony orchestras were organized. The best of European music was played on the programs, and American musical taste and standards improved, at least among the city folk who had access to concerts and recitals.

Sometime after Beethoven died in Germany, while central Europe was still producing the finest music in Europe, political upheavals brought about revolts, whose failure forced many Germans to flee to this country. Then for a time there was a strong German influence in American culture, which, after some years developed into a period when Americans, in their turn, felt that in order to achieve the best instruction in music they should go to Germany. Many German music-teachers came to this country, and naturally they imbued their pupils with admiration for the Fatherland. This is why compositions of the most important of the trained American composers of this time were written with the influence of European musical tradition.

For light-entertainment music, however, white singers and dancers saw fun in imitating the Negro's style of singing, dancing and joking, and a type of show came into use which was called the Negro Minstrel. It was an absolutely American style of entertainment which later achieved a vogue in England. The Negroes and the whites took each other's music, and interpreted it to suit themselves, and so created other "musics." There were Negro versions of white man's ballads, for they liked a song which told a story. *Casey Jones* is an example.

In these shows, the Negro minstrels were really white men blacked up. The entertainment consisted of

[35]

songs, both gay and sad, jokes, dancing, and "funny" business. It was all in imitation of the Negro; his happy-go-lucky disposition, the quaintness of his songs, his laugh, his humor. One of the most popular songs ever written by an American was *Dixie,* which was written by a Northerner, Dan Emmett, and was used as a minstrel "walk-around" in his show, *The Big Four.* The first minstrel groups were small—Dan Emmett's Big Four meant there were four entertainers in the troupe. But just as everything grew in the United States, so did the minstrels, and by the time Stephen Foster, our first most important song-writer heard them, the shows contained as many as forty entertainers. Then when a show was coming to town, the advertisements would read:

FORTY! COUNT 'EM! FORTY!
BIG! SUPERB! COLOSSAL! GARGANTUAN!

The black-faced entertainers would sit in a row, or sometimes two rows, in a slight semi-circle facing the audience. Some of them played instruments, banjos especially, and the two men at the end would invariably have tambourine and bones for percussion. They were even called Bones and Tambo.

The story of the minstrels goes back over a hundred years ago to a song-and-dance man named Thomas D. Rice—called "Daddy" Rice. He was a tall young man, an actor and comedian who was at the time engaged in one of the theatres in Cincinnati. He could tell a story, dance a hornpipe and sing in a way that was highly enjoyable. He had an eccentric manner, and was keen and shrewd to notice anything that might be turned to use in the entertainment of an audience.

One day as he sauntered along one of the main streets, he saw a battered, lame Negro stage-driver hopping around in the street to a song he was singing. It was *Jump Jim Crow*, the refrain of which is at the head of this chapter. "Daddy" Rice watched the driver, entranced both by the song and by the manner in which the colored man was delivering it. He thought that if he could imitate the peculiarity of the performance, it would make a good "act" on the stage. He decided that Jim Crow and a black face might tickle the fancy of the theatre-goers fully as much as the Irish red-nosed comedian singing his comic song. But his engagement was nearly over in Cincinnati, so that it was not until autumn that he had an opportunity of testing out his idea.

Then at the Old Drury Theatre in Pittsburgh he had a chance to introduce *Jump Jim Crow*.

There was a colored boy, named Cuff, who made his living by running errands for Griffith's Hotel, which adjoined the theatre, and by carrying trunks for passengers from the boats to the hotel. In this job, he had a competitor, another Negro boy named Ginger. Cuff also added to his earnings sometimes, by opening his mouth as a mark for boys to pitch pennies into it. It was Cuff who wore just exactly the battered clothes which "Daddy" Rice needed for his act. They made an agreement, and in the evening Cuff went to the theatre, disrobed, and loaned his clothes for the performance.

When the bell rang, and the opening music struck up for Rice's turn, Rice waddled on the stage, his face blackened with burnt cork, clad in a ragged old coat and wearing dilapidated shoes all holes and patches, a coarse straw hat, torn and bent, over a black, woolly wig. This extraordinary apparition produced a strange effect upon the audience. Rice began his ditty, introducing himself:

> Oh, Jim Crow's come to town, as you all must know,
> An' he wheel about, he turn about, he do jis so,
> An' ebery time he wheel about, he jump Jim Crow.

The effect was immediate. The novelty appealed, and a burst of applause greeted the introductory verse. With Rice's succeeding lines the enthusiasm grew, until the performer had to make up additional verses. For these he used news of local happenings, and sang about public persons in the town. The audience was delighted. Applause was deafening. There had never been such a demonstration there before. It seemed as if Jim Crow's improvisations would have to go on all night.

"Daddy" was still out on the stage, singing and dancing about, when Cuff, crouching under cover behind the scenes, heard the steamboat whistle. Steamboat was coming in with passengers, and Ginger would be down on the wharf and get all the business of carrying the trunks! Poor Cuff—he stood it as long as he could, but when the "act" showed no signs of ending and people were still applauding, he could bear it no longer. He protruded his face beyond the edge of the "scenery" and whispered loudly:

"Massa Rice, steamboat's comin'! Must have ma clo's!"

The appeal was useless. Rice did not hear it. He was out in the front of the stage, and as he had just made a happy hit at an unpopular city official, the audience was roaring with laughter. Cuff stuck his head out still farther, and called out, this time:

"Massa Rice. Must have ma clo's. Steamboat's COMIN'!"

Rice never heard him. But the audience, now seeing another "act" behind the real one, and all unknown to the actor, were beside themselves. The laughter and applause continued so loud, that the poor baggage-boy darted out on the stage, half-dressed, seized Rice by the shoulder and shouted,

"Massa Rice, gimme nigger's clo's. Steamboat's comin'!"

The incident brought down the house. The lights had to be extinguished before the audience could be persuaded to leave the theatre. And this is a story of the beginning of negro minstrelsy, which was a genuine American form of entertainment.

Rice appeared on the stage in England with much

success. His eccentricities as he amassed wealth, led him to wear five and ten dollar goldpieces as buttons on his coat and vest. He would snatch them off occasionally and generously present them to others as souvenirs.

It was this type of show—the Negro Minstrel—which Stephen Foster saw in Pittsburgh over a hundred years ago, in the days when he was a boy.

STEPHEN COLLINS FOSTER

All-American Song-Writer

Sometime over a hundred years ago, when boys and girls did not wait so long to grow up as they do now, a sixteen-year-old lad named William Foster went to work for a firm of merchants in Pittsburgh. Though he had been born in America, as well as his father before him, his ancestry, like that of the American composer Edward MacDowell, was Scotch-Irish. On both sides of his family he had relatives who had distinguished themselves in the Revolutionary War.

At that time, Pittsburgh was a pioneer town, which means that it lay on the edge of the white men's settlements, while beyond, to the west, the Indians still lived in the forests and still followed the great herds of buffalo on the plains. The first white men had landed two hundred years before on the eastern shores. Gradually they had pushed ever farther and farther across the west into the red man's domain and crowded him out.

The business of the firm which young William Foster joined, was general merchandising. They bought up all kinds of commodities to sell to the people who lived in these pioneer regions. In those days a person could not walk into a shoe store on Main Street for a pair of shoes, come out and go down the street to a hat shop, and then drop into the grocer's for sugar, as one does today. Very likely there was just one store on Main Street, and you would go there to supply yourself with everything you might need—from coal to coffee. Such a store would have to send someone down South to bring up the coffee and sugar, and someone else to the big cities of New York and Philadelphia for utensils and wearing apparel, such as frying-pans, shoes, hats, which were then being manufactured in New England's many little factories.

Since Pittsburgh was on a big river, it was the custom of the firm to load flatboats with the products of their surrounding country—furs, skins and flour, for instance—and float them down the Ohio and Mississippi Rivers to New Orleans, where the goods were either sold for money or exchanged for the Southern products which were needed in the North—such as cotton and sugar. William Foster was a diligent boy, for he became a partner to the men who had given him his job, and he went on these trips a couple of times a year.

It took a long time to float down the river on heavily laden flatboats. There were two possible ways of returning to Pittsburgh, and both of them required a long time, too. Sometimes Foster went back by land up through North Carolina, Kentucky and West Virginia—Indian country. There were no trains then, and he had to go on horseback. He could travel that way only when a large party were going together in the same direction, because the Indians were dangerous.

They had to carry arms and be ever on the lookout, ready for any surprise. At other times, Foster would go by boat, sailing around the Atlantic coast and up to New York. That way afforded its surprises, too. Once the vessel he was on was captured by pirates, but luckily a Spanish man-o'-war appeared just in the nick of time and frightened the pirates away. It was a close shave, which made a good story to tell in after years. In those early pioneer days, a boy or a girl could hardly help collecting a good many true stories of adventure. Their own lives were full of them. How their children would someday gather around them, wide-eyed, listening to the tales of what had once happened to mother and father when they were young!

When Foster returned North by boat, he would buy goods in New York and Philadelphia to take back to the Pittsburgh store. At first the goods were carried West on the backs of horses, but later they used Conestoga wagons, those "prairie schooners" or covered wagons, which now can be seen only in museums or sometimes in a movie. These wagons were often pulled by more than one team of horses, and each horse wore a string of bells attached above the collar. As the long line of wagons creaked and rattled over the rough roads, the bells kept up a comforting and merry jangling all the way across the mountains. Foster remembered those bells all his life.

On one of these trips William met a girl named Eliza Tomlinson, who was visiting her aunt in Philadelphia. Though he was on a business trip, he took the time to call on Miss Tomlinson with a bouquet of flowers. He learned that her home was in Wilmington, Delaware; that her ancestors had come from England. The more they talked the more they found to talk about. When he made a certain proposal to her, she said "yes" apparently, for they were married, later, at the home of other relatives of Eliza's in Chambersburg.

Girls had to be good sports in those days. In Eliza's case, she had to be willing to go on a honeymoon of three hundred miles on horseback, over the mountains, to an outlying spot where she had never been, and make her home there for the rest of her life. The Fosters' honeymoon took fourteen days, and Eliza was very tired on the last evening when they came in sight of Pittsburgh. But she said she liked it from the first, though it looked a dingy little town to her then; which meant that she must have been very much in love with William.

As the years went by, William Foster prospered and bought a large piece of land above the town. There he built what they called the White Cottage on a hill which commanded a fine view up and down the river. He even laid out a town, named it Lawrenceville, and gave property to the town. He and Eliza had ten children; and the ninth one—the one we are most interested in—was born in the middle of a great big celebration on a Fourth of July.

It was an extra-special Fourth because it was the

fiftieth birthday of the United States. Foster was a very public-spirited man, and he held the celebration in his woods back of the house. Bands played *Yankee Doodle* and *Hail Columbia,* and the crowds of people sang lustily. There were speeches and what was known as a "Bowery dinner." Some of the men fired off muskets in place of the firecrackers we now have. At noon there was a great burst of cheering for the Stars and Stripes, a salute from the cannon, and everybody sang *The Star Spangled Banner.* While the noise and excitement was going on in the woods, there was another and more quiet excitement inside the White Cottage, for that very noontime the ninth Foster child was born. It was a boy, and they named him Stephen Collins Foster.

That afternoon, in other parts of the country, the day was marked by the deaths of two great Americans: Thomas Jefferson and John Adams. Both had been presidents of the United States, and both had signed the Declaration of Independence.

The big family living at the White Cottage was furthered enlarged by having a colored "bound-girl" named Olivia Pise (nicknamed "Lieve"), and a "bound-boy" named Tom. Though Pennsylvania was adjoined by states where slavery was permitted, it was itself a free state. Lieve and Tom were not slaves, therefore, but it was understood that until they became of age they would work in exchange for having a home.

Lieve was a religious girl, and went to the church of a "shoutin'" Negro congregation. Now sometimes when young Stevie Foster didn't go to church with his family, he was allowed to go with Lieve to her church. As a contrast to the hymns that were sung from books in his own church, he heard, when he went with Lieve, a whole congregation make up their songs as they went along. It impressed the young boy profoundly.

Stephen Foster had a special love for music even when he was small. When he was only two and couldn't talk straight, he used to pick at his sister's guitar and call it his "ittly pizani." One day, when he was seven, he was taken into a music-store, and while there he picked up a flageolet which was lying on the counter. He felt it over, without anybody's noticing, and saw how it "went." In a few minutes, he surprised the bystanders by playing *Hail Columbia*. Later he learned to play on the flute, on the piano and even on the violin. At Lieve's church Stephen absorbed the feeling of the black people's music. He may have heard some of the mountain folksongs, too, when Lieve and Tom sang around the house while doing the chores. He may have known such songs as *Frog Went a-Courtin'*. He was fond of watching the Negroes loading and unloading the river-boats, hearing the roustabouts singing as they worked. Some of these songs must have been chanteys. But these songs, together with the hymns in church, and the spirituals and "shoutin'" in Lieve's church made up the young boy's musical background. When he was old enough to go to the minstrel shows, he heard the songs of white song-and-dance entertainers imitating the Negroes. In a pioneer town of a young country where the people were primarily interested in building up the wealth and strength of the country, there was small opportunity for enjoying the arts. Stephen was pretty well grown up before he knew anything about the musical tradition of Europe, or heard music of Bach, Beethoven, Mozart and other great composers. With no victrolas, radios, and very few concerts, where could he hear such music?

His interest in music was a puzzle to his father. Stephen had a sister much older than he, who was musical, and brother William sent East for a piano for her. It was brought over the mountains by horse and wagon. Mr. Foster liked music and even played a tune on the fiddle himself, occasionally. He thought music was fine for his daughter, but he hardly regarded it as a pursuit for a man. In fact, it was difficult for him to understand his son Stephen at all, and what he called Stephen's "weakness" for music. His mother, who had had opportunities to hear music in Eastern cities, may have understood her son's feeling for it a little better.

Another thing that made trouble was that Stephen was never a good student at school. He had no objection to study—in fact, he read and studied by himself a good deal. But he didn't like school and he hated the discipline. His first scholastic disaster happened when, at the age of five, he started off to school. Asked to recite the alphabet, he began bravely enough, suddenly stopped in the middle, yelled like an Indian and ran towards home a mile away. He never stopped yelling and running until he reached his destination.

He loved his home above all things, adored his mother, and had the happiest relations with his older brothers, William, Morrison, Dunning, Henry, and with his sisters. Whenever he was away from home, he invariably became homesick—except when he went to visit Uncle Struthers. A letter he wrote to his father when he was ten annoyed the boy because his lines ran uphill. He wrote to ask for some music:

> My dear Father:
>
> I wish you to send me a commic songster for you promised to. If I had my pensyl I could rule my paper or if I had the money to buy black ink but if I had my whistle I would be so taken with it I do not think I would write a tall, there has been a sleighing party this morning with twenty or thirty cupples. Dr. Bane got home last night and told us Henry was coming out here. I wish Dunning would come with him. Tell them both to try to come for I should like to see them both most two much to talk about. I remane your loving son,
>
> Stephen C. Foster

When he visited Uncle Struthers, however, he was content. Upon one occasion his sister wrote to William, "Stephen enjoys himself finely at Uncle Struthers'. He never seems to have the least inclination to leave there." And added, "Uncle just lets him do as he pleases with the horses and cattle, which makes him the greatest man on the grounds."

Uncle Struthers was a very old man then. He had

[48]

been a surveyor, hunter and Indian fighter—a real frontiersman. In his old age he had a farm in Ohio, which was still considered frontier and called the North-west Territory. He lived in a log house, and even then he continued to lead the night hunts for coons and pos-sums. Sometimes he took the boy along coon-hunting on moonlight nights. His tales of adventures with the Indians held Stephen enthralled. One day the old man could not find his small nephew. He searched all over —indoors and outdoors—but Stevie was gone. Finally, Uncle found him sitting in a pile of chaff up to his neck watching the chickens, turkeys and barnyard animals. When asked what he was doing, Steve answered, "Just thinking."

Uncle Struthers liked the boy, and recognized his unusual capacity for originality and musical talent. He prophesied that he would be "something famous if he lived to be a man."

Stephen much preferred lonely rambles to attend-ing school. He wandered in the woods or by the river. He was shy and not a good "mixer," yet with his own group of friends he could often be the funniest of them all. He was no sissy; he had plenty of courage and would pitch into a boy's fight as easily as anyone. His brother said Steve was cool and skilful in a fight, and that he could not stand bullies. At one school he had a friend a year younger than himself, and these two would sometimes play hookey and go rambling in the woods together. They would gather wild strawberries, and take off their shoes and stockings to go wading in a brook. When this boy grew up he said that Stephen used often to defend him in his bouts with his school-mates. Once later, when he was in his 'teens, Steve found two bullies at the end of the bridge, abusing and beating a drunken man. He jumped in and fought the weak man's battle for him, beat one of the bullies and drove the other away. In the fracas he received a knife wound on the cheek, the scar of which he carried all the rest of his life.

He was only nine when he and a group of boys made up a dramatic club. They fixed up a theatre in a carriage house. All the boys held stock except Steve. He didn't have to, because he was the star performer. The popular entertainments of those days were the black-faced minstrel shows, and the boys imitated them. When Steve came out on the stage and sang *Zip Coon, Long-tailed Blue, Coal-black Rose,* and *Jump Jim Crow,* he was always encored many times. He could put on a funny act. The boys gave three performances a week. They made enough to be able to go to Pittsburgh on Saturday nights to see the real shows and visiting actors. By this time father Foster had had reverses in money matters and the family lost their nice home. While Stephen was growing up the family moved several times, but always they lived in the vicinity of Pittsburgh—for some years in Allegheny City.

Moving around didn't help Steve's schooling, either. When he was tutored by a preacher who was not very strict in discipline, he got along better. But his education was always a puzzle to his parents. Stephen was unfortunate in not being able to hear first-class music while he was growing up, and in lacking the opportunity to study it. But neither he nor his parents ever dreamed that music offered both an opportunity for serious study and development, and a dignified and rewarding career. They never dreamed that the serious study of music would have provided the necessary discipline which Stephen needed, and through which he might have learned to order his life more happily. As he advanced up through the 'teens he was always groping for something he seemed never quite to grasp. As he never came to know much about musical theory, form, and harmony, he wrote out in songs the melodies which were always coming to him. They were the easiest and most natural form for him.

He wrote both the words and music, for he found it easier to make music fit his own words than those of somebody else. He had imagination and feeling, and what his father called a "strange" talent.

When Stephen was thirteen the family were again in a quandary about his schooling. This time brother William provided the solution. He was not Stephen's real brother but a cousin who had lost his parents when he was a baby, at a time when the Fosters had themselves lost a baby. They took their little relative into their own home, and he became fully as much of a son to them as if he had been really their own.

[51]

William was working in Towanda, and he offered to take Steve with him and put him in an academy in Athens nearby. The parents agreed, and in the middle of the winter the boys drove over three hundred miles in a sleigh behind two horses. Steve thought it was a wonderful trip.

It was while he was at Athens that Steve began to scribble down his music. He wrote a piece for Commencement and arranged it for four flutes. It was called *Tioga Waltz*. He played the first part himself, and the audience liked it well enough to want it played over. Again he became homesick, and he stayed only about a year at this school. After he returned, he entered Jefferson College, but that did not last long either. He did, however, study French and German, and his brother Morrison said that Steve used to like to paint with water-colors, too.

He was only sixteen when his first song was published. It was called *Open Thy Lattice, Love;* and was written for Susan Pentland, a ten-year-old friend. At that time the Fosters had no piano, and the Pentlands had, so Stephen went there to use their piano.

About this time the family discussed the idea of Stephen's entering West Point or Annapolis, which shows how far they were from knowing what to do for him. The Army or the Navy would be just the thing for some boys, but not for dreamy Stephen Foster, the boy who liked to sit by the hour and make up music on the piano. He loved to improvise accompaniments on

STEPHEN FOSTER

JOHN PHILIP SOUSA

VICTOR HERBERT

EDWARD MacDOWELL AT FOURTEEN

(*From a sketch by himself*)

ETHELBERT NEVIN

GEORGE MAILLARD KESSLERE, B.P.

WILLIAM C. HANDY

CHARLES GRIFFES

JEROME KERN

GEORGE GERSHWIN

IRVING BERLIN

GEOFFREY LANDESMAN PHOTO

ROY HARRIS

VICTOR KRAFT PHOTO

AARON COPLAND

JOHN ALDEN CARPENTER

BARRETT GALLAGHER PHOTO

DEEMS TAYLOR

RICHARD RODGERS

the flute when his sister or his friends sang. If only he had had someone to guide him who could have pointed out to him his real goal in music and could have given him definite aims, how hard and happily he could have worked.

With a group of intimate friends about him, Steve liked to make music in an informal way. At evening parties with the boys and girls he had always known, he was happy sitting at the piano and singing with them. He had a ringing, baritone voice capable of a plaintive sweetness that could bring tears to the eyes of his listeners. He would sing in choruses when concerts were given for charity, but he hated all pretense, and he would not go near the piano if he thought someone wanted to show him off. Once, when he was eighteen, an old family friend was preparing to give a large party and all the Fosters were invited. When Stephen heard that the lady had said, "Tell Stephen to bring his flute with him," that was the end of his going to the party. He said:

"Tell Mrs. —— I will send my flute if she desires it."

Brother Morrison used to sit in the room evenings listening to Steve playing and singing to himself. He said that Steve used to cry while he sang and played. Morrison also said that melodies danced in Stephen's head continually. "Often at night he would get out of bed, light a candle and jot down some notes of a melody on a piece of paper," then go back to bed and sleep.

There was a club of young men, when Stephen was nineteen, which met twice a week at the Fosters' house, to practice "songs in harmony." They called themselves "The Knights of the S. T." (That may have meant the square table, but nobody knows since it was their secret.) Steve led them in the singing, and he was very exact about it. They sang all the Negro songs which were popular then, and they wanted more. So Stephen began to write songs for them.

The first song he gave his club to sing was *Louisianna Belle*. They liked it so well that Steve was encouraged to write *Old Uncle Ned* in the following week. Encouragement was what he needed. It was not long before these songs became well known in Pittsburgh, the people having learned them from each other—the way folk songs were learned.

Whenever traveling troupes came to Pittsburgh, Stephen and Morrison went to see the plays. Sometimes there were plays of Shakespeare, with very good actors. Thus the months passed and Stephen was twenty. Even though people were singing his songs, neither he, nor certainly his father, thought of song-writing as a possible life's work. His father thought it was high time Stephen got to work, instead of giving in to his "weakness" for music.

It was decided that he should go to Cincinnati and be a bookkeeper for his brother Dunning, who was in business there. One day the family and friends went down to the boat to see him off. For three years Stephen

Foster stayed there keeping books orderly, neat and businesslike in Dunning's office, while in spare time he wrote songs. Fortunately Cincinnati has always been a musical center, and there probably was more opportunity of hearing music. At least, it was while Stephen was there that something happened which gave him the idea, for the first time, that he might make a living by his music. A man whom Foster had once known as a music-teacher in Pittsburgh, was now a small music-publisher in Cincinnati. He was the man who had published *Jump Jim Crow*. Stephen gave him two of his own songs, *Old Uncle Ned* and *Oh! Susanna*. The songs were published and sold so well that the publisher made ten thousand dollars—enough to set himself up in a big publishing business. Stephen, not realizing the worth of his songs, had given them away, so that all he received was a few free copies.

However, he became known. He was asked to write songs especially for various minstrel troupes. He was sought out. When a New York publisher wrote to him asking for songs, Stephen Foster began to experience the sweet sensation of growing fame. The visiting minstrels knew him; he now belonged to the inner circle, and was greeted in the theatre. No need now for him to buy entrance tickets, he could just walk in. The troupes began to advertise his songs. Four songs published as *Foster's Ethiopian Melodies* were *Nelly Was a Lady*, *My Brudder Gum*, *Dolcy Jones* and *Nelly Bly*. When Stephen was twenty-three the great gold-rush to

California began, and *Oh! Susanna* was adopted by the Forty-Niners as a kind of theme song. It was sung all the way across the continent—and back again. The visiting European piano virtuosos, Herz and Thalberg, took the *Oh! Susanna* melody and played concert variations upon it.

Stephen Foster was successful at last. His success seemed to come all at once. Everybody was singing, humming or whistling his songs. There was now no need for him to remain in a business office struggling with bookkeeping when his heart was in his music. After three years, he returned home. There he made himself a studio in a back room at the top of the house. He shut himself up to study, and to work earnestly at the business of supplying songs to the New York publisher. An arrangement was made by which Foster was to receive three cents on each copy sold. He worked so seriously that he would permit no one to come into his studio except his mother.

By this time many of the girls and boys he had grown up with were married. While he was living in Cincinnati, he once made a visit home to attend the wedding of Susan Pentland, the girl for whom he had written his first song when she was ten. Her husband had been one of the Knights of the S. T.

The English novelist, Charles Dickens, was once in Pittsburgh during his American visit. He became ill there, and was attended by Dr. McDowell, the father of Jane McDowell who was also in Stephen's circle of friends. Dr. McDowell used to be driven around to make his professional calls by his old Negro servant, Joe. Old Joe, when not driving the doctor, had house duties as butler. Many times he opened the door to "Miss Jenny's" admirers. With his scuffling walk and a broad grin on his face, he would go to her and announce her callers, giving her their bouquets of flowers.

Jane McDowell was a very beautiful girl, with auburn hair and eyes to match. Stephen was one of her frequent callers, and there came a time when he fell in love. He said later that it was Jane's hair that did it. One evening when Joe admitted Steve to the house, Stephen said to him, "Some day I am going to put you in a song."

And he did. But it was years later when the inspiration came for writing *Old Black Joe*, and the real old black Joe was gone.

It was a very embarrassing evening when Stephen put Jane to the test. Stephen had just arrived, when Old Joe announced another caller, Richard Cowan (also a Knight of the S. T.). Jane must have confused her dates that evening. But Stephen was there first and he had no intention of leaving. When Richard came in, Stephen merely turned his back, picked up a book, sat down under a light and pretended to read the whole evening. He probably just sat and stared at the book and never read a word. He had enough to ponder over. Richard Cowan was wealthy, handsome and distinguished-looking. He was already a practicing lawyer

and in a position to marry. Stephen, though pleasant-
looking, could not be called handsome—he was rather
on the short side; and he certainly was not wealthy.
No doubt he was thinking bitterly how much finer a
figure his knightly adversary appeared to Jane than
did he. In disposition, he was always mild and gentle,
but that night he was standing no nonsense. After what
must have been a very strained evening, the end came
at ten-thirty which was then the outside limit for calling hours. Richard stood up to leave, and with an
elegant gesture of wrapping his military cape around
him (for in those days, men wore capes just as much
as they wore coats), he bowed low towards Stephen's
back, and said:

"Good evening, sir."

Never a word from Stephen; he went on sitting.
Jane saw Richard to the door, and returned to the parlor,
knowing that a crisis was at hand. But she really did
not know, she admitted later, whether her sympathies
lay with Richard or with Stephen. However, she was
given no time to think. As she entered the room,
Stephen was standing by the table, pale and stern.

"And now, Miss Jane," said he, "I want your
answer! Is it yes, or is it no?"

That would probably take a prize in sudden pro-
posals. But apparently it was the right way for Stephen
to have handled the affair, for it was Stephen whom
Jane married. The evening's "huffiness" was of short

duration, too, since after the marriage Steve and Dick Cowan remained good friends.

Now that Stephen Foster had, at twenty-four, become "something famous" as uncle Struthers had predicted, songs came from his pen more often. Because at first he wrote songs that were used by the minstrels, his words were written in Negro dialect. The first song with the words written as those of a white man, was *Old Folks at Home*. He wrote humorous songs with nonsensical words after the Jim Crow type, such as *De Camptown Races* and *Oh! Lemuel;* sentimental parlor songs so popular at the time, *Old Dog Tray, Hard Times Come Again No More;* love songs such as *Gentle Annie, Laura Lee* and *Come Where My Love Lies Dreaming*. Several of his songs were inspired by Jane, as: *Jeanie with the Light Brown Hair,* and *Jenny's Coming o'er the Green*. He wrote some hymns also. Of his 188 songs, the one which has been translated into the greatest number of foreign languages, and heard all over the world, is *Old Folks at Home*.

He began to write the verse "Way down upon the Pedee River," but he was not satisfied with the name of the river. One day he went into his brother Morrison's office, and said:

"What is a good name of two syllables for a Southern river? I want to use it in this new song of *Old Folks at Home*."

Morrison asked him how "Yazoo" would do. But Stephen said:

"Oh, that has been used before."

Morrison then suggested Pedee. The composer said:

"Oh, pshaw, I won't have that."

Then Morrison took down an atlas from the top of his desk, and they opened it to the map of the United States. Finally, Morrison's finger stopped at a little river in Florida. It was the Swanee.

"That's it," cried Stephen, delighted, "That's it exactly." And he went out of his brother's office without saying another word.

Though he was never in Florida and never saw the Swanee River, Foster had some river trips into the deep South. He and Jeanie "of the light brown hair," together with some of their old friends who were now married—some of the old Knights of the S. T.—journeyed down river as far as New Orleans. Foster visited a beautiful Kentucky "mansion," belonging to a cousin, which had been built in Revolutionary times. It is said that this lovely home with its happy well-cared-for slaves, was his inspiration for *My Old Kentucky Home*, and that these glimpses into Southern life produced such songs as *Massa's in de Cold, Cold Ground*.

(The writer of this book was dining one summer evening in 1936 in front of a café in Bruges, Belgium. Across the medieval square of this old city, the ancient Tower rose into the sky. The sun set and as the evening became darker, the carillons began their pealing from the Tower, in a recital by a distinguished carilloneur. The second half of the program was given to American airs, in honor of the visitors from across the sea. One of the numbers on the program was misprinted: "Massa's in de Gold, Gold Ground.")

Foster loved his songs, but he always realized the shortcomings of his musical training and his lack of technical knowledge of composition. Perhaps this was partly why he was too modest for his own good and never asked enough for his songs. Perhaps also it was because he cared little for money—though that fact made life harder for Jane and the people nearest to him.

The various minstrel troupes of Foster's day vied with each other in introducing new songs. One of the best-known companies was that of E. P. Christy, who conducted popular Negro melody concerts. For such small sums as fifteen dollars, Foster sold to Christy the permission to have the first use of some of his songs. Christy's Minstrels were the first to sing *Oh! Boys, Carry me 'Long,* and *Old Folks at Home.* Foster also sold to Christy the right to have the latter song published under Christy's name. Stephen Foster didn't mind, and for a long time it was supposed that Christy had written the song. Foster gave permission for it when he was thinking of writing a different type of music, and felt that he might not wish to be known solely as a writer of Ethiopian songs. Later on, he did wish to acknowledge *Old Folks at Home,* and to have his name appear as its writer.

Once a friend of the family gave Foster a handsome setter dog, which became his constant companion. The Fosters lived on the edge of a park then, and Stephen used to enjoy watching the dog playing with the children in the Common. It was this dog whose faithful friendship he remembered in *Old Dog Tray*. Sometime later he owned another dog, a homeless mongrel which he had picked up in the street. He named it "Calamity" because of its mournful howl.

At first, Stephen and Jane Foster lived with Stephen's family. After they had a little girl of their own, they moved to New York. There Foster had the opportunity of hearing orchestral and choral works, but it was an opportunity which for him came too late. Though he made enough money for his family to live on for some years, he had no idea of how to build up reserves against a future day. He lived without plan according to the dictates of his emotions, and this led, naturally, to a sense of dissatisfaction with himself, and the procedure of his life became unsettled and unhappy, until it ended in tragedy.

He was always giving in to his streaks of homesickness. After about a year in New York, Stephen Foster was seized with a sudden nostalgia, and he returned one day to tell his wife to pack up, they were going home. In twenty-four hours they had sold their furniture and were on their way to western Pennsylvania. They arrived at night—unexpected. They rang the doorbell and Stephen's mother awoke and came downstairs. She knew his step on the porch, and, as she was passing through the hall, she called out:

"Is that my dear son back again?"

Stephen was so affected by hearing her voice, that when she opened the door, he was sitting on the little porch-bench, weeping like a child. Except for business trips to New York, or an occasional pleasure trip, Foster never went away from home again so long as his mother lived.

This was hardly flattering to Mrs. Stephen. It is not well for more than one family to live together, and she may have felt hurt to realize that she and the little girl Marion did not seem to fill Foster's life enough to make his home complete. There were times when they lived apart. When Stephen did not earn enough to provide for his little family, Mrs. Stephen worked to help herself. In those days it was unusual for a married woman to work outside her home. Today a woman is admired for being able to work at outside interests while she oversees a home, but in those days no one did it unless she had to. This also added to Stephen Foster's sense of dissatisfaction with himself. When Foster's parents died and brother Dunning, too, and many of the others moved away, Stephen Foster seemed lost. His only anchor had been the home wherein his mother lived. When he had that no longer, he was set adrift.

He returned to New York. It was not long before an unhappy desire for drinking overcame him. He struggled against it, but the craving was too strong for him. At the beginning of the Civil War, the Fosters were again living in New York. The little Marion was eight years old. Some one passed Foster in the street and described him as "a short man, who was very neatly dressed in a blue swallow-tailed coat and high silk hat." But before many years he ceased to look neatly dressed. There was a period when his songs did not come so easily, and as time went on, his wife returned to Pittsburgh to find work for herself. Her husband was left alone in New York. He became subject to spells of ague, and was no doubt really ill.

Suddenly in his middle thirties, he began to turn out many songs again. It was at this time that he wrote *Old Black Joe*. Some of the others were *Virginia Belle, The Merry, Merry Month of May, Our Bright Summer Days are Gone*. His last song was *Beautiful Dreamer*. Toward the end of his short life he sold his songs for almost nothing. He seemed to feel that he didn't need much. He ate very little, taking no interest in food. Gradually he came to take less and less interest in his clothes. He felt forlorn, and he looked forlorn. He spent much time in the back of an old tumble-down grocery store in the Bowery, at the corner of Hester and Chester streets.

A young man named Cooper wrote the words for some of Foster's songs in these days, and Stephen called him "the left wing of the song factory." Cooper said that Foster was never intoxicated, although he drank constantly. As he did not care for food, he would often make "a meal of apples or turnips from the grocery shop, peeling them with a large pocket-knife." He said that Foster wrote with great ease, without the aid of a piano. If he had no music-paper, he would take whatever he could find—brown wrapping-paper if there was nothing else; and after ruling lines upon it, he would proceed to write down a melody, for he always had one in his head.

One winter morning Cooper received a message that his friend Foster had met with an accident. He dressed quickly and hastened to the hotel where Stephen Foster was living. He found his friend, fallen on the floor, cut and bruised. He sent for a doctor. Foster was sent to a hospital, and there he died. In one of his pockets was found a little purse containing thirty-eight cents and a small slip of paper on which was scribbled in pencil:

> *dear friends*
> *and gentle*
> *hearts.*

Some years afterward, the great singer Nillson came to America. Soon after her arrival she heard *Old Folks at Home.* She was "so much struck by its plaintive melody and touching words that she immediately set herself to learning both." After that she almost always sang the song in her concerts.

While Foster was alive this song had traveled to

many countries. Not many years after it had been written, a gentleman was on a walking-tour through the Scotch borderlands. There he heard Foster's songs being sung by the shepherd boys and girls, along with the ballads of Burns and Ramsay. He said that in a gathering, after the bagpipes had droned out the great ballads *Scots wha hae wi' Wallace Bled,* and *Lord Athol's Courtship,* a voice would begin an American (Foster) melody and all would join in. The songs were known as Foster's American Melodies. They were sung as far away as China, Africa and Australia.

An interesting story which illuminates the quality of Foster's songs was told by a Scotchman. When he was a boy, and a student in Glasgow, he practiced Foster's tunes on his tin whistle, but he never knew that the songs had been written by a man named Foster. He said that a school banquet was never complete without singing some of Foster's songs, but they were taken for granted, as folksongs are, and no one knew that Foster, an American, made them sing. He said that a change came over the atmosphere of any occasion when the orchestra struck up the notes of Foster's "old-time melodies."

Foster was a true son of the United States. No other country could have produced him. He sang about his own land and his own people. His songs have the simplicity, sincerity and humanizing quality of folksongs. There is nothing difficult about them. Their harmonies are the simple tonic, dominant, sub-dominant.

Their sentiments about home, friendship, loyalty, love, are understood by everybody. The appeal is universal. His language was the language of the heart of the common people.

In 1940, seventy-six years after his death, Stephen Foster was nominated as one of the Americans to be ever remembered in New York University's Hall of Fame. He is the first musician—and so far the only musician—who is there enshrined.

Stephen Collins Foster, born in Pittsburgh, Pennsylvania, July 4th, 1826. Died in New York City, January 13, 1864; buried in Pittsburgh.

JOHN PHILIP SOUSA

The March King

When John Philip Sousa was growing up in Washington, the nation's capital, where he was born, he heard a great deal of band music. It was a thrilling time to hear bands, and an unusually thrilling place to hear them, because it was during the Civil War. Band music is always most exciting when patriotic feelings are stirred up, and they are most stirred up in time of war. Young John Philip was, like all boys, moved in the marrow of his bones by band music. Good or bad, he loved it all.

His own father, Antonio, played trombone in the Marine Band, and since John (or Philip, as his father called him) was exceedingly fond of his father and respected him highly, this fact no doubt had something to do with the lad's preferences. We are all apt to think that what our father does is extra good. Still, there is hardly a boy in the whole world, or a girl either, who is not fascinated when a band goes marching up the street.

Antonio Sousa was a Portuguese, but when his family had to flee from a revolution in Portugal, they went to Spain, and Antonio was born in Seville. Later he went to England, then came to America. In Brooklyn, he met a Bavarian girl who had come to visit the United States. Her visit lasted the rest of her life, because she and Tony Sousa were married. During the years that followed they had ten children, and the oldest was John Philip. It was natural that he had to begin early to make his own living when there were so many younger ones growing up, and from the time he was a young child he wanted to be a musician.

However, his own music lessons got off to rather a bad start. It came about in this way: An old friend of his father's, also a Spanish gentleman, was in the habit of calling frequently upon the Sousas. One evening, during his visit, Philip persisted in rolling a baseball around the room, disturbing the conversation of the grown-ups. The gentleman, who was a retired orchestra player, said that perhaps a few lessons in solfeggio might be good for the boy. He knew instrumental music, but alas, he had an atrocious voice for singing. At Philip's first lesson with this gentleman, he could distinguish no difference in the old man's tones. Every tone he tried to sing sounded like every other tone. Philip said the only difference was, that "when he was calm he squawked; when excited, he squeaked." At the first lesson, the gentleman wanted Philip to sing the syllables of the scale after him.

"*Do,*" squawked the would-be voice teacher.

"*Do,*" squawked Philip in imitation.

"No, no, sing *Do,*" and this time he squeaked.

[69]

"Do," squeaked Philip, trying his best to imitate the very sound he had heard.

No wonder lessons like these left the boy worn out. He would have preferred to be out playing baseball.

It was this same gentleman's son who opened a conservatory of music in the neighborhood where Philip lived. When the boy was seven, he was enrolled among sixty pupils, and began the study of violin. There were to be more stormy times with this teacher, the son of the old squeaker.

Philip overheard Professor Esputa (the violin teacher) tell Mr. Sousa that even if Philip didn't learn anything it would at least keep him off the streets. Philip was piqued by this remark. As a result, he never opened his mouth to volunteer any answers for the first three years he was in Mr. Esputa's classes. The teacher could not tell whether the boy was learning anything or not. But all this time, since Philip was very eager to learn music, he was drinking it all in. Finally, at the end of three years the first examinations were held.

Five medals were offered by the school. Imagine everyone's surprise when Philip won not one medal, but all the five medals! Mr. Esputa was in a quandary. He told Mr. Sousa that he could not possibly give all the prizes to his son, for fear of what the other pupils would say. Mr. Sousa, a sensible man, laughed and said he was glad enough to know that his son had won them, but that it would not make him any smarter to

[70]

have them, and the teacher might make better use of the medals if he could. Esputa gave three to Philip, and two to other pupils. Though John Philip Sousa was to have many great honors conferred upon him throughout his life, and though medals were awarded to him by kings, he always kept the three little golden lyres given to him by Mr. Esputa. They reminded him always, he said, how he had fooled everyone by his silence, and impressed upon him that "silence is truly golden."

There came a time in his eleventh year, when he was to play as soloist in one of the academy's annual evening concerts. By that time he was already earning money by his playing, so that he was not nervous at all about playing. Had he been a little nervous, he might not have done what he did, for on the day of the concert he did a foolish thing. It taught him a lesson.

The very day of the concert he was scheduled to pitch a game of baseball. When he arrived home, hungry, tired and dirty, he found the household all upset; his mother was ill, his eldest sister away on a visit, and the maid had gone out. He had to clean up, get out his Sunday clothes and be content with a sandwich. But—he could not find a clean shirt. The laundry had not come back.

He hurried over to the Conservatory to tell his teacher, who said:

"That's all right, run over to my wife and tell her to give you one of my shirts."

This being done, Philip was pinned into a man-sized shirt by Mrs. Esputa.

Now in playing violin it is impossible to keep the arms still. Both arms are raised, and the right arm is constantly moving about with great movements.

As Philip was playing, one by one the pins worked loose and came out. The collar, which was pinned together at the back, came open and began to creep up the back of his head. The shirt fell away from his neck. The laughing audience and the dropping shirt made the soloist forget his notes. He rushed off the stage, and sought a dark corner in which to hide. He was so mortified, he wished he was dead.

After the concert, the teacher and pupils were invited for refreshments of ice-cream and cake. Philip, trying not to be seen, was nevertheless discovered by Mr. Esputa, who said to him:

"You have made a nice mess of it. You should be ashamed of yourself and do not deserve any refreshments. You should not have spent the afternoon playing ball, but should have prepared yourself for the more important work of the evening."

There was no ice-cream for Philip. It was a lesson he never forgot, and he said that ever afterwards he either worked or he played, but he never tried to do both at the same time.

There was an affair with that same teacher which taught the boy another kind of lesson, a lesson in sympathy and thoughtfulness of others.

As you doubtless know, it is difficult for a teacher to be always in a calm, happy frame of mind. For instance, it is impossible for a teacher to put off a lesson just because he has a headache, or because he wants to go to a party, as pupils sometimes do. Once, Mr. Esputa was suffering from boils, but he had to go on teaching even though he felt miserable. Aside from the pain and discomfort, boils will make a person very short-tempered. At this time, during his lesson, Philip did nothing to assuage his teacher's bad humor. Instead, he felt more sorry for himself, because it seemed that he could do nothing to please his teacher that day. When Mr. Esputa stopped in the middle of the lesson and told Philip to draw a long bow, Philip said he was drawing it as long as he could. This made the teacher angry, he felt that he was being contradicted. Instead of trying it again, Philip started to argue and say that his arm was already up against the wall, whereupon the teacher flew into a rage. He drew back his right arm with a grand sweep holding his own bow, a very valuable present which had been given him, and in so doing struck the bow against a piece of furniture. It broke in half.

"Get out," he shouted, and that was the end of Philip's lesson for that day.

Poor Philip. He felt that he had done nothing to deserve such treatment, and when he reached home his father noticed that something troubled him. When he inquired, Philip told him the whole story. His father said:

"Well, I suppose you don't want to be a musician. Is there anything else you would prefer?"

"Yes," said the boy, and his heart was sad, "I want to be a baker."

"A baker?"

"Yes, a baker."

"Well," considered Mr. Sousa, "I'll see what I can do to get you a position in a bakery. I'll go and attend to it right away," and he went out of the house.

In a little while he returned and told his son that he had seen Charlie, the baker two blocks away, and Charlie had said he'd be glad to take Philip and teach him how to bake bread and pies. He went on to say that he wanted his son, however, to be more educated than most bakers were, for he felt that he would then surely have a better chance later on to improve himself financially. He said that Philip must continue with school while he learned baking but he could give up his music. The baker, he added, was ready to start Philip that evening at eight-thirty.

Philip went to the baker's at eight-thirty. They worked all night. Early in the morning he helped load the wagon and went out with the driver to deliver bread. He was very much impressed because the horse knew the front doors of all the customers' houses. About eight in the morning he was through and went home to breakfast. He had had about a half-hour's sleep during the night.

At the bakery when the bread was in the ovens, the workers could take a short nap while it was baking.

That afternoon after school, Philip didn't feel much like playing baseball. He went home and hung around listlessly until supper was over and it was time to return to the bakery. Again it was the same kind of night, except that he thought that the baker and his wife were not so kind to him as they had been the first time. The next day he learned nothing at school, and when evening came he dragged himself off for his third night at the bakery. This time the baker snapped at him to do this, do that, and once he had to run upstairs and rock the baby, crying in its cradle. He was so worn out that he fell asleep while the baby was still crying, and Mrs. Charlie came up and slapped him awake. After delivering bread the third morning, he returned home completely tuckered out. When his father said, "How do you feel this morning?" he fell sound asleep before he could answer. Then his father asked Philip's mother to give him breakfast and put him to bed and let him sleep all day. That evening he said to Philip:

"Of course you want to be a baker, don't you, Philip?"

"No," wailed the boy, "I'd rather die than be a baker!"

"Then," said his father gently, "I think you had better make it up with Esputa and start in with your music again."

Forever after, Philip and his teacher were the best

of friends. He studied hard, worked on orchestration, harmony, and sight-reading. Though his father tried to teach him to play the trombone, Philip could never make a "go" of it. The neighbors could not put up with his trombone practice, either. But the band in which his father played, sometimes permitted the young-ster to play cymbals with them, or the triangle or the Saxhorn, so that as early as ten years of age, he knew what it felt like to play in a band.

By the time he was thirteen John Philip Sousa had organized his own quadrille band. Except for himself, the players were grown men. He played first violin himself, and the band had a second violin, viola, contra-bass, clarinet, cornet, trombone and drum. They played for dances, and Philip began to attract notice as a violinist.

One day while he was practicing a concerto, there was a rap on his door. He opened, to see a gentleman who said he had been listening for five minutes to the playing and had knocked because he wondered who the player was. Philip invited the man to enter. The man complimented him on his playing and then asked him if he had ever thought of joining a circus. Philip said he hadn't. The gentleman then said that he was leader of a band in the circus that was at the time playing in Washington, and if Philip wished, the leader would get him a place. The idea appealed to Philip. A circus would no doubt appeal to any boy. He said that he would like it, but he did not think that his father would approve. The man suggested that Philip go ahead with it without telling his father. But Philip knew better than that, and besides he liked his father too well to leave without telling him. The circus man then suggested that perhaps fathers just did not know what a future there might be for a boy traveling with a circus.

After further persuasions, the man suggested that as they were going to strike their tents the following evening, Philip go along with them. After two days he could write his father and tell him what a good time he was having, and then his father would probably not interfere. Philip agreed. Warning him to keep it secret, the man took his departure.

The more he thought about it, the more wonderful it all seemed to the boy's imagination. He would follow the circus and make money, and perhaps some day he would become the leader of a circus band himself. It was too good not to tell anyone about it, so he confided in his friend, Ed, who lived next door. Ed very likely told his mother, who regarded the venture from a different viewpoint, and she, in her turn, very likely told Mrs. Sousa.

The next morning while Philip was still lying in bed dreaming of conducting a circus band under a monster tent, he was roused by his father's voice.

"Good-morning, Son."

"Good-morning, Father."

"When you dress today," said his father, "put on your Sunday clothes."

[77]

What was up? wondered Philip. It wasn't Sunday. However, he breakfasted in his Sunday clothes, and then his father said, "We'll take a walk."

They walked in the direction of the Marine Barracks. It was the ninth day of June, and that day his father enlisted young Sousa in the Marine Corps as an apprentice boy to study music until he should outgrow his infatuation for the circus. He knew that his thirteen-year-old son would never desert from the Marine Corps to run away with a circus.

It was about that time that Philip heard some music which was an experience he never forgot. He heard a most excellent musician, Theodore Thomas, play *Träumerei* on the violin. It was to him the most beautiful music and the most beautiful playing he had ever heard. For the first time the idea struck him that the most wonderful thing of all would be to write music— music to lull and charm the listener.

As the years sped by, Sousa played more and more with musical organizations while he was growing up. He played first violin with the Orchestral Union and at the same time studied violin, piano and harmony with the conductor. He was introduced to musicians and music-lovers. One of the latter was also a patron of chamber music, who every Tuesday evening had a string-quartet group play in his home. He invited young Sousa to join the group. It was at these evenings Sousa came to know the chamber works of Haydn as well as very rare works of older masters, the music of which had been ordered especially from European music stores.

This music patron, upon Sousa's request, secured his release from the Marine Band through the Secretary of the Navy. Then he tried to persuade the young man to go to Europe to complete his musical education. At that time, it was felt that if an American wanted a thorough education in music, the only thing to do was to go to Germany for it.

Sousa informed his new friend that it was impossible for him to go to Europe, since his father couldn't afford to send him. The elder Sousa had too many younger children to provide for. When the gentleman met this objection by suggesting that Sousa call on a philanthropist whom he knew and who, he felt sure, would be glad to give money to educate a talented young musician, Sousa would not consent. He did not wish to be obligated to anyone. It was against his feeling of pride and independence to accept money in such fashion. He remained in America for his education, and, as an elderly man, said he never regretted it, for as a result he could call himself a "truly American musician."

Pupils came to him and he began to compose. One set of waltzes he gave away to another man to publish under his own name. The man was no musician, but he was in love and thought he might win his girl with music! Sousa's next two pieces were marches, which he sold not for money but for a hundred copies of each.

There were times when he became discouraged in his studies because he felt that the lack of musical atmosphere in his home was a hindrance to him. His mother was unmusical, and his father, though he had played trombone, was not a good technical musician. Then, too, teacher Esputa was a hard task-master, who was kind only to his girl pupils. With the boys he was severe and stern. Perhaps one reason for Sousa's eagerness to take advantage of every musical opportunity, and starting early to do so, was his great need for encouragement.

He jumped at the opportunity to conduct in a theatre when he was called on suddenly because the regular conductor had gone away. He could read music at sight, and with time for only one rehearsal, he went through the performance. He was so eager to make good that he was at the theatre three hours early. Then one evening the conductor at the opera house was taken ill. Sousa was sent for. He could be relied upon. After this came his first real offer, and he became leader of an orchestra for a show that was going on tour.

Before Sousa was twenty-five, the Gilbert and Sullivan light opera *H.M.S. Pinafore* was the rage in the United States. Since there were no international copyrights then to protect the authors, there were dozens and dozens of companies playing the Gilbert and Sullivan operettas and never paying a cent of royalties to the authors. One day Sousa was told that a group of society amateurs wanted to do *Pinafore,* and that he might have the chance of drilling them. Since they paid very well, and there was an opportunity for a long run, Sousa was glad to do it. The next evening, when he went to begin the engagement, he found the "finest set of voices and beauties" he had ever met. He said:

"Being young, I was extremely stern at rehearsals. It is wonderful the amount of drilling competent people will take. Only the stupid, vain ones, who are ill-equipped for the work anyway, get 'hot under the collar' at correction or reproof. When we finally gave our performance it created a sensation." It was still playing the following year when Gilbert and Sullivan came over to America. They heard it and Sousa was made very happy by the kind remarks of the composer, Sullivan.

On the 22nd of February one of the "beauties" introduced Sousa to her understudy, Jennie Bellis of Philadelphia. He thought she was the "loveliest little girl" he had ever seen. He liked everything about her, "her manner, her speech, her face, her voice." She told him that she was celebrating two birthdays, Washington's and her own. She was just sixteen. Before she was seventeen, Sousa married her.

After writing a musical comedy and conducting it on tour, there came finally the position in which Sousa made the reputation for which he is known today. He became leader of the Marine Band; leader of the band in which he had played and studied as a boy. He must then have been thankful that his father interfered and prevented him from running off with the circus.

His first care was to build up the music-library for the Band. There was no new music in it. Everything was out of date, and badly arranged for instruments, and he found nothing good about it. The first thing he did was to get good music; then he drilled and rehearsed his men constantly.

The Marine Band is the official band of the President of the United States. When an orchestra is needed at receptions and functions at the White House, the Marine Band is the orchestra. When there are parades, or when concerts are given at the Capitol, it is the Marine Band which plays. At special functions when ambassadors of foreign countries are present, and courtesy requires a delicate recognition, the Marine Band must be ready with the national airs of the countries represented. Sousa was always ready with his special music. He collected the national airs of all lands for their music-library. His published collection includes patriotic and typical airs, not only of the great countries, but also of the small far-away places such as Samoa, Lapland, Abyssinia, and even the songs of many tribes of American Indians. The melodies of the Apache, Cherokee, Chippewa, Dakota, Eskimo, Iowa, Iroquois, Vancouver tribes appear in Sousa's book of national airs, all harmonized so that the band could play them. Perhaps the Indians themselves might not recognize their wild tunes tamed to our harmonic rules, but at any rate, Sousa went to the trouble of collecting them from ethnologists and people who had lived and traveled among the Indians.

For years, at the White House receptions, when cabinet ministers, ambassadors, generals and admirals were assembled in the East Room to greet the President, it had been the custom for the band to play *Hail to the Chief* to announce the entrance of the President himself. At one of these affairs, President Arthur left his guests and went out in the corridor for a word with Sousa.

"What piece did you play when we went in to dinner?" inquired the President. Sousa replied,

"Hail to the Chief, Mr. President."

"Do you consider it a suitable air?"

"No, sir," answered Sousa, "it was selected long ago on account of its name, and not on account of its character. It is a boat song,* and lacks modern military character either for a reception or a parade."

"Then change it!" ordered the President.

Sousa then composed the *Presidential Polonaise* for indoor affairs at the White House, and the *Semper Fidelis March* for outdoor reviews.

Under the auspices of a newspaper, the *Washington Post,* prizes and medals were offered one summer for the best essays written by pupils in the different grades of the public schools. A great day was planned in June, and part of the exercises was to be a program of music by the Marine Band. One of the proprietors

* *Hail to the Chief* is an old Scotch boating-song.

of the newspaper asked Sousa to compose a march for the contest and to play it for the first time on the day the awards were to be made. For this occasion, Sousa composed and played the *Washington Post March*, which became so popular that it was played all over the world. On the day when it was first played, all the children of Washington must have been there to hear it. The trees around the band-stand were filled with boys who had climbed up to be near the music. At the first strains of the *Washington Post March*, the High School Cadets came marching up the street amid the cheers of all the assembled children. It was a great day for Washington's children. Later on, Sousa also wrote a *High School Cadets March*. Once on tour, when he used to receive all kinds of requests to play certain favorites, he was much amused to have a note handed to him asking for the *Ice Cold Cadets!*

As an example of how the *Washington Post March* spread over the world, there is the story about the Army major who, years afterward, was walking in the jungle in Borneo. Suddenly he heard sounds of a violin in the forest. It was playing the *Washington Post March*. He followed up the sound and came upon a native boy scraping away on his fiddle with a sheet of music pinned up before him on a tree.

Dancing-masters seized upon this tune for launching a new dance. It was called the "two-step"; but when Sousa later went to Europe he discovered that in

England and in Germany the dance itself was called the "Washington Post."

After John Philip Sousa had drilled the Band into an organization of which he was very proud, and after he was satisfied with its repertoire of good band music, he wanted to take the band on tour so that it might play to people outside of Washington. A patriotic celebration in the town of Fayetteville, North Carolina, commemorated the so-called Mecklenburg Declaration of Independence. The Marine Band was sent to take part in the ceremonies, as the President was unable to be present to deliver a speech. A committee of prominent citizens selected a chairman who discussed with Sousa the musical program for the occasion. Sousa said:

"Well, we will open with the *Star Spangled Banner.*"

"Quite right," agreed the chairman.

"Then we will play the *Coronation March* from the opera *The Prophet,* by Meyerbeer. We will follow with the *Overture* from *William Tell; On the Blue Danube;* excerpts from *Aida;* and then, *My Country 'tis of Thee.*"

"That is all very fine," said the Southerner, "but I should like to remind you that there's a tune down here that we love like mother's milk. I don't know whether your band plays it, but we surely would like to hear it."

"What is it?" Sousa's voice sounded rather unconcerned and discouraging.

"It is called *Dixie.*"

"I know the tune," said the bandmaster. Then he

[85]

added, "I'll think it over, whether we can make use of it or not. You know we are a very artistic organization and must always consider our programs very seriously."

"Yes, yes," drawled the poor chairman, "but if you can tuck it in, I know the people would love to hear it. Some of them haven't heard it since the Surrender."

Sousa, always keenly aware of the value of a dramatic moment, saw his opportunity. He said no musician would think of going South without *Dixie* in his repertoire.

At the ceremonies people flocked in from the mountains and farms until the town was crowded. They slept in covered wagons, and Sousa even saw some boys asleep in drygoods boxes, under stoops and on benches. It was a big time in Fayetteville.

The Governor made the first speech, after which Sousa's band stood up and played the national anthem. It was politely and quietly received by a crowd in good behavior. Then the Chairman made a speech to introduce the Senator who was the "idol of the State." As the Chairman sat down and before the Senator began his speech, Sousa quickly signaled to his men, and they charged right into *Dixie*. He said it was like an electric shock. A great yell began in the grandstand, and "went booming down the street, through the surging crowd." Hats went flying. Old men cried. Women hugged each other, and for fifteen minutes the ceremonies were held up.

How strange it is that a melody can so tie itself around our hearts.

During the week the band was in Fayetteville, their programs were always something like this:

> Overture, *William Tell*
> Song,   *Dixie*
> Waltz,   *Blue Danube*
> Song,   *Dixie*
> Airs from *Faust*
> Song,   *Dixie*
> Medley, *Favorite Tunes*
> Song,   *Dixie*

"And the encore to every one of those numbers," said Sousa, "was—*Dixie.*"

Yet *Dixie* had been written by a Northerner, Dan Emmett, and was first sung in a minstrel show in New York during the Civil War.

After Sousa had been leader of the Marine Band for twelve years, having seen service under five presidents, he asked for his release. He wanted now to organize a concert band of his own. It was not long before he had his own band ready to play at the World's Fair in Chicago. There he had a great honor and an experience which he cherished ever after. His band played with the great orchestra led by Theodore Thomas. This was the man whose playing of *Träumerei* on the violin many years before in Washington had inspired young Philip to compose. Sousa's band had prepared its part of a work, called *Columbus*, written by an American composer, John Knowles Paine. It was a march and hymn for orchestra, military band, and chorus. At the rehearsal Sousa was happy to have his labors recognized when Mr. Thomas said:

"I thank you for the pains you have taken."

They went out to lunch together and sat in the restaurant until after six in the evening—two musicians in sympathetic mood. Sousa said, "It was one of the happiest afternoons of my life. Thomas was one of the greatest conductors that ever lived." The band leader told Thomas that his early dream of heaven was Thomas's playing of *Träumerei* on the violin, whereupon the conductor's eyes grew wistful, and he said, remembering, "that was some pianissimo."

The *Gladiator March,* which Sousa said was his first hit, he offered to a publisher for fifty dollars, and it was returned. Then he sold it for thirty-five to a publisher who had paid the same amount for *Semper Fidelis, High School Cadets* and other marches. At first it was the publisher who made his fortune from the Sousa marches, and not the composer. He was able to buy two factories: one for making reed instruments, and one for making brass instruments, entirely on what he had made from the Sousa compositions. It makes one think of Stephen Foster who gave away his songs *Old Uncle Ned* and *Oh! Susanna* to a man who made ten thousand dollars from the two songs and set himself up in a music-publishing house. Foster received a few free copies of his own songs! But Sousa learned and thereafter sold no more marches outright. From the *Liberty Bell March* he received more than thirty-five thousand dollars in royalties.

During a long and busy life, Sousa wrote over a hundred marches, besides waltzes, fantasias, operas, suites, songs, as well as books, including an interesting story of his life, and a story for children, called *Pipetown Sandy*. But it is for his marches that he is chiefly remembered, and he seemed to be able to write a march for any occasion. With his famous band, he toured the United States many times. Through these tours he became the most beloved and most popular of American musicians. It was an "event" when Sousa came to town. Sometimes the mayors proclaimed holidays in honor of his visits, and flags were flown. He made several tours of Europe with his band, and once took them around the world.

While in England the first time, Sousa and the band were asked to play for His Majesty King Edward VII, the grandfather of King George VI. The King wished it to be a surprise performance for the occasion of the Queen's birthday. It was kept secret even from the men in the band. They had no idea they were to play for royalty until they had taken a train ride to Sandringham, one of the King's homes in the country. On his program that evening, Sousa played in addition to several of his own marches, his collection and arrangement of hymns of the American churches, and also plantation songs and dances. The King asked for seven encores!

[89]

Then he presented Sousa with the medal of the Victorian Order.

A little brass-band journal published in England printed an article saying that Sousa was as much entitled to the name of "March King" as Johann Strauss was to the title of "Waltz King."

As the vessel steamed out of the harbor on Sousa's return from his first trip abroad, he paced the deck thinking of all the things he had to attend to when he reached New York. Suddenly inside his brain he felt the rhythmic beat of a band playing. A melody took shape and kept on playing within him during the whole voyage home. He could not get it out of his head, he was completely possessed by it. Upon reaching home he wrote down the imaginary band piece. He never changed a note from the way he had heard it inside his head, day after day, while crossing the ocean. It was the most popular march he ever wrote, *The Stars and Stripes Forever*. It attained the status of a national march. A Frenchwoman once told Sousa that the march "sounded to her like the American eagle shooting arrows into the Aurora Borealis."

Sousa considered the English audiences "the best listeners in the world." He wrote, "perhaps the music-lovers of some of our larger cities equal the English, but I do not believe they can be surpassed in that respect. Reputation-building in the musical world would be a pleasant task among the educated English. In England, audiences were always fair and often wonderfully enthusiastic." He thought that an Englishman "judges a composition according to its musical worth alone."

Once Edward Bok, then editor of the *Ladies' Home Journal*, offered Sousa five hundred dollars and the copyright if he would make a new setting for S. F. Smith's verses, *My Country 'tis of Thee*, which are sung to the tune *God Save the King*. But Sousa wouldn't do it. He felt that no music, good, bad or indifferent could take the place of the tune which the public had associated with those words for so many, many years.

By the second time the Sousa band went to England, the leader had written a complimentary march for His Majesty which he called *Imperial Edward*. The band played for the King at Windsor Castle this time, and Sousa was told that when the children heard he was coming, they prepared to play their own concert of Sousa band records on the gramophone in the nursery. They were not permitted to attend the real concert in the great hall in the evening. One of those children became King George VI of England.

On that evening Sousa was informed that the King was very anxious to hear the American national anthem at the close of the program. Therefore Sousa had instructed his men that our anthem was to be played, and that, at the end of it, they were immediately and without a break to go into *God Save the King*, beginning very, very softly and make one long, great crescendo to the end. The program came to a close, and after the applause, there came a fitting silence. Then Sousa brought

[91]

his men to a standing position. The signal was given. As the soaring phrase of the *Star Spangled Banner* sounded forth in the great hall of Windsor Castle, the King arose and stood at attention. The audience arose with him. At the end of the phrase . . . "and the home of the brave" the band drew out the long notes, *diminuendo*. Then so quietly that it could scarcely be heard, the very notes changed into the opening of the British anthem, *God Save the King*, which is to Americans, *My Country 'tis of Thee*. Sousa was facing the King and saw his countenance change. As the music swelled in volume, it seemed to Sousa that the King was thinking: "These aliens are asking God to protect me and my country." Sousa felt that, "in the splendor and solemnity of the moment he seemed to be glorified." Having been the band leader for five presidents of the United States, Sousa felt very sure that a great position glorifies a man, that the grave responsibilities of high office lifts a man even above his own average.

The story of another concert given in England shows the ability of the bandsmen. They had given a concert at the Shakespeare Memorial Theatre at Strat-ford-on-Avon soon after their arrival in the country on one of the tours, and at the last minute the Countess of Warwick asked them to play for her guests at Warwick Castle near by. But as they were completely booked up she suggested that they give her a midnight concert. It turned out to be a stormy, wild night of wind and rain. Finally the band arrived in its several automobiles, but the car which contained all the music went skidding down a hill completely out of control. The music never arrived until the concert was over. The band had played everything from memory.

Although nearly everyone came to know what Sousa looked like, the famous band-leader once went into a bank in Buffalo and was not at first recognized. The band had been playing there for a week, and the band's manager, having received a check for several thousand dollars, went with Sousa to the bank to cash the check. The cashier said to Sousa:

"You'll have to be identified."

Thereupon the bandmaster turned his back to the cashier. He raised his arms and started to conduct an invisible band, while whistling *The Stars and Stripes Forever.* The clerks burst out laughing and applauding. One of them whispered to the cashier, and the check was cashed!

In the summers whenever he was free from tours and conducting his band, Sousa followed his hobbies. As a boy he used to go hunting with his father. Though he liked to hunt ducks, deer and quail on the preserves in South Carolina, he liked trap-shooting best. He preferred to shoot clay pigeons rather than live ones, and clay-bird shooting was his favorite sport. As a marksman he was known as a dead shot. He also liked riding, and one summer during World War I he started off on a thousand-mile horseback journey. At home he kept his own riding horses.

In the spring when he was sixty-two years old, he received word from his friend, John Alden Carpenter, another American composer, that the band at the Naval Station needed help. Would he come? He went, of course. The result was that he joined the Navy as a lieutenant in charge of the music. He formed a band battalion of 350 men with its commander, musical director, and surgeon, and then he organized bands for each regiment at the Naval Station. He was able to send bands to ships or stations whenever and wherever they were wanted. His own band played in Red Cross drives, and Liberty Loan drives during the War, and raised millions of dollars.

When he was a young man leading the Marine Band, Sousa already wore a heavy beard. He thought it made him look foreign. American musicians did not have much chance in those days. Americans thought only foreigners could have musical ability, and many American musicians tried to look like foreigners. Sousa really thought his beard had helped his career. As he grew older, judging from his pictures, the beard was trimmed more and more. Finally, during the war, the beard disappeared altogether. Sousa used to say that his beard won the war. He explained this by adding that when the Kaiser heard that he had shaved off his beard, he quit, declaring that it was useless to fight a people who would make such sacrifices! But the real reason was probably his age. When he joined the navy at sixty-two, there was a rule that no one over forty-seven could be accepted. But, there was just one Sousa, and the Navy needed him. Perhaps he thought that if he removed his beard, he would look younger than forty-seven!

During his long experience of having his own band, Sousa saw the numbers of American musicians increase more and more. When he assumed the direction of the Marine Band as a young man, there were not more than half a dozen native Americans in the band. Twelve years later, when he organized his own band, he tried to have them all Americans. If the best players of their respective instruments were foreign-born, he used them, but as time went on, most of his bandsmen were Americans. He was very pleased when some of his early bandsmen sent their sons to play under him.

Sousa was very jolly and humorous. He was a genial host and hated, more than anything, to have to dine alone. His personality was magnetic; people were attracted to him. Though he could be stern and strict when directing, his men were very fond of him. The band had a spirit of comradeship. When the band numbered eighty and sometimes a hundred men, they had their own ball teams, and played games for their recreation.

Perhaps if Sousa had gone abroad for study as a boy, when he had the opportunity, he might never have been the "March King." He might have turned into another kind of composer. The harmonies he used were usually simple tonic, dominant, sub-dominant; the kind which learned, academic musicians feel are used exclusively only when writers do not know much music. These were Foster's harmonies. But there is no need for every musician to be profound. Sometimes the learned, musical schoolmasters forget that the real attraction in music is the spirit, not just the notes. Sousa's marches have a zip and a lift which puts heart into marching men. Many a time a Sousa march has enlivened the tired, aching feet of men who have had to march through dreary hours. The rhythms and melodies are joyous. Sousa's own feeling was that "entertainment" in music was of more real value to the world than a technical education in musical appreciation. Certainly it is the value which comes first. A child will be "entertained" by music long before he ever has any idea of how "good" the music is. Sousa always arranged his programs with the entertainment value in mind. That is why he was so popular. Entertainment is more popular than learning.

Once in Germany he was told that his band played well enough but that the music was too *sugary!* That was a silly remark, because it conveyed the idea of comparisons. Some people like candy, some like pickles. There is no comparison. One can like both—at different times, of course!

Sousa did not like the violent tone of the Helicon tuba which was at first in use in the Marine Band. It was a large instrument which wound round the player's body. The player had to pull it down over his head.

He suggested to an instrument-maker a tuba with a large-sized upright bell, so that the sound would, as he said, "diffuse over the entire band like the frosting on a cake." The instrument was made, and it is still used, and called the Sousaphone.

It was Lieutenant Commander Sousa who invented the phrase "canned music." He never felt that "canned music" would take the place of personal appearances of musicians. In his middle seventies, when he was informed that his world-famous march might be leading troops from a motor, equipped for carrying mechanical music, he asked:

"Will the truck keep in step, too?"

Sousa did not believe that there is any nationalism in music. He felt that composers who have been called writers of national music, were merely interpreting themselves and their own reactions to life. Perhaps he was right. A man in Norway for instance would naturally have different feelings about a snowy landscape from the man who lived in a jungle on the equator. These two men would also feel very differently about airplanes. Sousa said, "You cannot bound a melody as you would a country. Music may have many dialects, but its language is universal." In his many travels he found that people's emotional reactions were the same regardless of geography. He said that when he played humorous music, the laughs always came in the same spots, whether he was playing to an audience in Spain or in a town in North Dakota.

He had a happy, busy life and he wrote happy, busy music. He did not like to play dark, sad music, but if the occasion demanded, he could furnish it. He thought that perhaps his success was due largely to the fact that he and his band "played chiefly sunshine music." For, as Sousa said, "that the world needs always."

John Philip Sousa, born in Washington, D. C.
November 6, 1854. Died in Reading,
Pennsylvania, March 6, 1932.

VICTOR HERBERT

*"Always do the best you can, no matter what
the work may be."*

A hundred years ago there was an accomplished
Irishman named Samuel Lover who was never forgotten
by his grandson. Lover was a painter, a poet, a song-
writer, a singer, a dramatist, a humorist, a musician, an
actor and one-man entertainer, a writer of grand-opera
and comic-opera librettos, and a novelist remembered
for his book, *Handy Andy.* It is no wonder that his
grandson always spoke of him with pride. He had,
moreover, a wonderful memory for a melody, and this
was also an ability of Victor Herbert, the grandson, who
never forgot a melody that he once heard, though he
could not always place its origin.

There is an interesting story of how Samuel Lover
used his extraordinary memory for music in enabling
him to paint a miniature of the greatest violinist of his
time, Paganini. The violinist had a most unusual personality and strange appearance. He was tall, thin,
gaunt, with a great nose and a white, colorless face
topped with a mop of wild, black hair. His playing of
the violin was marked with such amazing feats of virtuosity that some people felt that he must surely have
been gifted with supernatural powers, and that only the

devil could have played with such fiery spirit. When Paganini played in Dublin, Samuel Lover was eager to paint this extraordinary-looking musician. The violinist consented to the sittings, but during them he seemed dull, and the painter tried to arouse a liveliness and animation in his face. He said to the violinist that he very much liked a *caprice* motive from one of his concertos, and he proceeded to hum it. Paganini looked surprised, and said:

"You have been in Strassburg?"

"Never."

"Then how did you hear that air?"

"I heard you play it."

"No—not if you were not in Strassburg."

"Yes—in London," insisted the painter.

"That concerto I composed for my first appearance in Strassburg and I never played it in London," insisted the violinist.

"Pardon me," Lover went on, delighted at having aroused a spark of interest, "you did—at the opera house."

"I don't remember."

"It was the night you played an *obbligato* accompaniment to Pasta."

"Ah, Pasta! . . . Yes, how magnificently she sang that night."

"And how you played!"

Paganini accepted the compliment, and went on:

"But the motive! Yes—I did play it at the time,

but only that once in London. You must be a musician.
It is not an easy air to remember."

"It was encored, Signor," explained Lover graciously, "and so I heard it twice."

"Ah, so. But still I say it is not easy to remember
except by a musician."

Some years after this time, Samuel Lover lost
money by being over-generous to a friend, and in order
to earn more money quickly, he decided to come to
America. America has ever been the refuge for people
of other countries who have wanted either freedom or a
chance to earn money. Lover had introductions to a
number of people, among others, the American writer,
Hawthorne, and he therefore received a pleasant wel-
come.

Soon he arranged to give an entertainment. The
tickets were a dollar. The hall was crowded with the
"beauty and fashion of the city" and many people were
turned away. The *New York Herald* reported:

"At eight o'clock, Mr. Lover made his bow to the
audience and was received in a most cordial and flattering manner. It would be difficult to describe the nature
of the entertainment so as to do it justice. We will content ourselves with saying that it was a flow of polished
witticisms, puns, songs, jokes and recitations, combined
with touches of deep pathos, delivered in such a felici-
tous style that the audience was at one moment completely besides themselves with merriment and another
almost melted into tears. All the songs were of his own

composition and indeed, all new to this country except two or three. . . ."

Mr. Lover's American visit of two years was a great success. He toured the cities with his "Irish Evenings," as he called his entertainments, and then returned to England and made his home at Seven-oaks, not far from London. For some time he continued giving entertainments, and he then used his American experiences by giving "American-Irish Evenings." Afterwards he settled down to write and paint for the rest of his life.

His daughter, Fanny, had married Edward Herbert, and two years after their son, Victor, was born in Dublin, Mr. Herbert died. Then Fanny took her son to Grandfather's house in England. That is why Victor Herbert, though Irish, never lived in Ireland except for a short time when he was a baby; and also why he always remembered his grandfather instead of his father.

In his grandfather's house, the boy heard much music. His own mother played the piano beautifully, and among his grandfather's guests were many musicians. Young Victor heard Irish folksongs from the time he was in the cradle. Mr. Lover used to take his grandson on his knee and tell him stories of America; about the wonderful city of New York, and the magnificent Niagara Falls.

When it came time for Victor to go to school, Mr. Lover advised his daughter to take the boy to Germany because he felt that there they could find better education more cheaply. He was also thinking, perhaps, that he didn't want his grandson to become too English. Though he himself preferred to live in England, he was a staunch Irish patriot and wanted his grandson to be the same.

Mrs. Herbert agreed, and packing two portable bathtubs with her luggage, (which amused the Europeans), she and her young son, Victor, set off for the south of Germany, and came to live in a town on the shore of beautiful Lake Constance. There Mrs. Herbert met and married a German physician, and the family moved to Stuttgart. In this way the Irish boy who was someday to live in America and there become a composer, received his education in Germany.

He went to school and wanted to shine in his class. He enjoyed games, and when his mother suggested that he take lessons on a musical instrument, he didn't want to be bothered. Perhaps it was because he had a stepfather who was a doctor that it was settled that Victor should study for the same profession. He was agreeable enough, and never once did he think of being a musician.

But there was a very fine cellist who often visited the house, and Victor's mother thought it would be wonderful if her son would learn to play the instrument which was capable of giving such glorious and mellow tones. In her estimation, her son *ought* to learn to play at least one instrument. But he would have none of it. The cello would take too much time, and after his studies he wanted some time left over for games and fun. He might have gone on and become a doctor before he ever found out that he should be a musician, except for something that happened which brought Victor around to his mother's wishes.

In preparing for a festival, the school band discovered that it needed another flutist. Victor Herbert was asked to fill the place, and to learn in two weeks the piccolo part of the overture to Donizetti's *The Daughter of the Regiment.* When he once decided to do it, he got to work. And how he worked! Two weeks only in which to learn not only a part for public playing, but how to play the instrument.

He did it. The festival came off and the piccolo played its part, but what a two weeks for his mother! The constant shrill piping that went on in the house, when she much preferred the low, deep tones of the cello! Then, too, she thought what a ridiculous instrument it was for her strapping big son to play—a tiny pipe. However, it was the beginning of Victor's music.

Sometime afterwards he became acquainted with a boy who played violin. He liked his new friend's playing, and when the friend echoed Victor's mother's opinions about piccolo players, Victor at last informed his mother that she could buy him a cello. In one way, Victor had been right, for he said afterwards, that from the time he began to study the violoncello his school work suffered. He was no longer among the first five in his class.

He was about fifteen or sixteen when he started to practice the cello. Through the influence of the father of his violinist friend, Herbert became the only pupil of one of the finest concert cellists of the time. He lived for over a year in his teacher's home, which gave him excellent advantages. His teacher's eye was on him constantly, and since he could never fall into bad habits in his playing, his progress was constant and rapid. It was not long before he was able to play in the orchestras. In this way his education advanced as he played under the leadership of the greatest musicians—Liszt, Brahms, Rubinstein, Saint-Saëns, Delibes.

For some years Herbert traveled about Europe playing in orchestras, and sometimes playing solo in concerts. Once in Dresden, he went into the theatre before playing time, and began to strum on the piano. He had never studied piano but had just picked up enough by himself to play a little. Another musician of the orchestra came over to him and said:

"You should compose."

It was probably the first time that such an idea ever entered young Victor Herbert's head. He doubted if he had it in him. But the other felt sure of it, and told Herbert not to waste time but to begin composing. Shortly after that, Herbert was made first cellist of the Court Opera in Stuttgart; and then, remembering the advice of his fellow-musician, he began the serious study of composition under a professor who gave him a thorough grounding in harmony, counterpoint, and

[105]

orchestration. At the same time, he was told to arrange old melodies for cello and orchestra. When that was finished, he was told to write a suite in five movements —also for cello and orchestra. This was good enough to be played in public, by the time he had studied composition only four months.

Victor Herbert was always capable of hard work. When he once began to compose, he never stopped. At the same time, he knew how to enjoy himself, and during the years in Stuttgart as cellist of the Court Opera, he became one of the popular young men about town. He was large, with an imposing figure, good-looking, gay, cheerful, generous, and always ready with a good story.

When a new soprano came to the Opera, a handsome girl with a statuesque figure as well as a beautiful voice, a romance sprang up between her and the first cellist, and they became engaged.

At this point, a young American conductor named Walter Damrosch came from New York in search of singers for the Metropolitan Opera House. Voices and artists capable of singing the Wagner roles, which were to be a new feature at the Metropolitan, were what he wanted. After hearing the new singer, the American gave her an offer to come to New York. Instead of jumping at the chance the artist said that since she was engaged to be married to Mr. Herbert she could not possibly accept. The surprised Mr. Damrosch investigated Mr. Herbert. Then he made another suggestion to the singer. Would she come *with* Mr. Herbert, if he could be the first cellist of the Metropolitan orchestra? Ah, that was a most agreeable arrangement. The singer and the cellist were married, and soon afterward they came to New York. Victor Herbert was twenty-seven at the time.

He liked America fully as much as his grandfather had, and he stayed for the rest of his life. He bustled about and was a true American go-getter. Wherever there was need for a cellist, there was Herbert. He played with the Philharmonic Society under the leadership of Theodore Thomas, the conductor so much admired by Sousa. Herbert himself greatly admired Anton Seidl, who was conductor of German opera at the Metropolitan. His own good playing and all-round musicianship drew Seidl's attention, and Herbert became Seidl's assistant conductor in the summer concert season at Brighton Beach. He taught the cello at the National Conservatory at the same time that Dvořák was there. (Edward MacDowell's mother was secretary for the Conservatory.) Herbert played with chamber-music groups also, and won a very high reputation as a cello player. Sharing his desk in the orchestra of the Metropolitan was a cellist who was to become the grandfather of Ferde Grofé, the "arranger" for jazz music.

When Herbert had been in America for seven years he was invited to become the leader of Gilmore's Band in New York after the famous bandmaster Gilmore had died. (In his time, Gilmore's Band had the highest reputation in America, and Gilmore himself was an early idol of that other famous bandmaster, John Philip Sousa.) This was the beginning of Herbert's step away from serious music. Because of his experience playing with the Metropolitan orchestra under Seidl, his bandsmen considered Herbert an admirable and thorough musician. Undoubtedly he had learned much about conducting under Seidl's baton. He was very strict at rehearsals, demanding good playing, and he used to scold his men roundly if he thought they were not giving him worthy results. But if he sensed their fatigue at long or difficult rehearsals he would stop everything and put them into good humor by telling them an amusing story. His men always liked him. Later, when he became conductor of the Pittsburgh Orchestra, his men there were equally fond of him. They always regarded him as "one of the boys." When Herbert's birthdays came around, the men of the band or orchestra would appear outside Herbert's house and serenade him. On St. Patrick's Day they all wore green neckties in honor of his Irish origin, of which Herbert was always proud.

Victor Herbert was fond of pomp and good living. To live well was, in fact, one of his main objects in life. He liked to spend money and to see money spent. He had as great a talent for making friends as for making music. He became "the favorite everywhere." One of his friends said that with Herbert music and friendship were everything. When his band and orchestras went on tours, the leader appointed a tuba player especially to look after, and to keep replenished, a large wicker lunch basket. The tuba player received a special allowance for this duty. It was inconceivable to Herbert that he could ever miss a meal, or do without his favorite foods and drinks. He enjoyed food so much that he would never allow a discussion of business matters to disturb his dinner. He appreciated fine cooking, and nothing irked him so much as the little tidbits he sometimes encountered at ladies' *musicales* when moneyed amateurs engaged him and other men of the orchestra to help them in playing chamber music. He wanted food to be excellent—an event in itself, and the talk that went with it to be agreeable and gay.

As bandmaster, Herbert was very fond of his uniform and liked marching in parades at the head of his men. He was delighted that his band was selected to play for President McKinley's Inaugural Ball. It was the period when great balls were in fashion, when hosts and hostesses vied with each other in arranging the most splendid and magnificent affairs when many thousands of dollars were spent on an evening's entertainment. Herbert's band played for the dancing at one such ball in New York which was intended to outshine all previous balls. He loved magnificence. A vain man, contented only when at the top of his particular group, Herbert sometimes came in contact with jealousies thus aroused.

Though Herbert's dearest wish was to be known as a composer of grand opera, and though he did write

[109]

and see produced two grand operas of his own, he is not remembered for them now. He had been in America eight years before beginning on the career which won him a place in the musical history of the United States as a composer of operetta.

Herbert's own temperament was well suited to lighter music. He composed serious music—even Dvořák praised his violoncello concerto—but it was never so successful as his light music. Seeing that a composer could be successful in America only in the field of light music, he became more and more interested in music for the theatre. Observing how the light operas of Offenbach and Sir Arthur Sullivan were winning great applause and bringing large incomes to the pockets of their respective authors, Herbert decided to write comic opera until he had enough money to permit him to write whatever he wished. The result, naturally, was that he wrote light operas for the rest of his life.

In that kind of music he found his true niche when he was in his middle thirties. Charming melodies flowed easily from his brain and he used to fancy that he resembled Schubert, of whose music he was extremely fond. He was so versatile that in conducting he could instruct his men in four different languages, switching instantly from English to German, Italian or French. Likewise in his operatic writing he could work on several scores at once.

Before a musician can write an opera of any kind, however, he must have a libretto—unless like Wagner he can write his own. Herbert had composed chamber music, a cantata for the Worcester Festival, a *Serenade for Strings* and had received good notices which increased his reputation as a versatile musician; but he was still unsatisfied, and often said to his friends:

"I wish I had a good comic-opera libretto."

Through a commission to write music for an event at the Chicago World's Fair, Herbert came in closer contact with the stage. This particular event for the Fair had been planned on a scale so large that it never took place, but not long afterward, through those connections, Herbert found the libretto which he had been wanting. His first produced operetta, *Prince Ananias*, appeared in New York when Herbert was about thirty-five. It was a failure. Nevertheless, it was a beginning, and Victor Herbert was not one to be discouraged by a failure. The following year saw his first successful one, *The Wizard of the Nile*. Critics wrote unfavorably about it, called the music "trivial," and "imitative," but the public liked it. Later it was played in England, Germany and Mexico.

He became conductor of the Pittsburgh Symphony Orchestra; and for six years, while constantly playing and rehearsing daily the finest kind of orchestral music, he was finding spare time in which to compose the light music of his choice. One of his popular operettas, *The Fortune Teller*, was composed the year he went to Pittsburgh. His reputation for versatility pleased him, though he was often criticized by people who thought it was impossible for a man to interpret the serious classical music well if he himself preferred writing in a light vein. It also pleased him to have a reputation for hard work. He was proud of his contact with the great musical figures such as Richard Strauss and Kreisler who visited Pittsburgh to appear with the orchestra. Andrew Carnegie, one of America's music patrons, was an ardent admirer of Victor Herbert, and used to say of the Pittsburgh Orchestra:

"My idea of heaven would be to hear Victor Herbert and his men play for me twice every day."

But his path led back to New York where he devoted his energies more and more to writing music for the theatre. Some of his early compositions were turned down by a New York publisher, who told Herbert to "stick to his orchestra job and leave composition to composers." Later, he was to be glad to publish Herbert, and the man he advised not to compose was to become known as America's favorite composer.

Most of Herbert's composition was done on order, and he seems never to have refused an order. There was one season when he engaged to write four operettas: *The Singing Girl, The Ameer, Cyrano de Bergerac,* and *The Viceroy.* He wrote them all at once. In his studio he had three low desks and one tall bookkeeper's desk. At the latter he could write standing when he grew tired of sitting. The scores were spread open. As the Muse moved him, he jumped from one to the other. These pieces dealt with four distinct periods, places, and sets of characters. The scene for *The Singing Girl* was laid in Germany; *The Ameer* in Afghanistan; *Cyrano de Bergerac* in old France; *The Viceroy* in Venice. To help his moods in their constant changing, Herbert kept a small washtub filled with ice in the room, and on the ice he had bottles of beverages to fit each operetta.

Besides four operettas, he wrote chamber music and a symphonic poem that year. He loved to work. He never forgot the musician in Dresden who had first said to him, "You should compose." Composing was as easy for him as making friends and he accomplished a great deal of writing in his lifetime. There were frequent failures sprinkled among the successes, but Herbert was a hardy soul who could stand it.

An artist who straddles two fields is always open to more criticism. This is due to the jealousies of people or critics who have hard enough time understanding an artist's output in one. Herbert's associates in serious music resented his successes in the popular field. But his associates in the popular field—the show-business end of Tin Pan Alley—were proud to have a man who, as they said, "knew his business." There was never any arranging to be done on Herbert's tunes. He did his own. He thought orchestrally. He did not compose at the piano, in fact, he could not play piano well. When he did, he tried to make all the instruments of the orchestra sound as he heard them, and the piano did not suffice. But in orchestration, he was so adept that he could write the parts, if they were needed in a hurry, before writing the score.

Sometimes Herbert was accused of using melodies which were really not his. Because of his prodigious memory, it was no doubt difficult at times to differentiate his own original tunes from something which was stored away in his memory. Occasionally, upon playing a new tune for a friend, he would ask, anxiously, "Where does it come from?" though later he admitted that he had often "borrowed" material from the masters.

The *March of the Toys* from Herbert's *Babes in Toyland,* has been one of his most frequently played orchestral pieces on the radio.

As he wrote on order, Herbert almost always knew, while composing, who would be the singer to introduce his songs. His opera *Babette* was only a moderate success for him, but the singer, Fritzi Scheff, who sang her début in this piece, had great personal triumph. The applause for her was enthusiastic. She was so happy that she pulled the composer-conductor up on the stage and gave him a hug and kiss before the delighted audience. The next day the newspapers made the most of that hug and kiss. And it would appear, that, in a way, Victor Herbert did, too.

Two seasons later, the same actress appeared in what became the most popular of all Herbert's shows, *Mlle. Modiste*—the greatest success of his career, for from it came the hit song, *Kiss Me Again.* It is interesting to track down the melody which became so popular, and since Herbert himself told the story of its beginning, we can repeat it.

Victor Herbert was conducting a series of concerts out of town, he said, when the librettist of *Mlle. Modiste* came to see him—to tell him that he had written it and that he thought there should be one special melody to stand above all the others. Moreover, it should be, in his opinion, an ingratiating song for Miss Scheff. Herbert tried, but said, "We couldn't make any headway. Little melodies came to me, but not one that seemed to be the kind needed. . . . The orchestra and the concerts were uppermost in my mind." Several days passed, and the composer grew more and more perturbed. Finally, he decided to "put on pressure," saying to himself that it was foolish not to concentrate hard on the thing, for if he did not concentrate he would never find a melody.

"That night," he said, "I had the matter in mind when I went to bed. Suddenly the melody came to me. I rose and turned on the gas. Then I jotted down the thirty-two bars that were my inspiration. I felt I had conquered. Then I went to sleep."

But in after years, Herbert's publisher wrote a postscript to the story. The song did not appear as *Kiss Me Again* in the operetta. *If I Were on the Stage* was an ensemble number. The scene depicted the emotions of a prima donna, (sung by Fritzi Scheff) and in it, said the publisher, one line of melody stood out—the last line of the chorus, "Kiss Me Again." The publisher persuaded Herbert to develop the excerpt into a full-sized song and write a complete new melody for the first part. The rewritten version with words supplied by the librettist, made the song a "hit," and the sales jumped from seven thousand copies to a million.

Many years later, Herbert heard a crooner crooning *Kiss Me Again.*. He was outraged at this "mangling of a man's work." It was the direct incentive for his activity in helping to organize an association of authors, composers and publishers to protect themselves.

When Herbert's operetta, *The Red Mill,* opened, the manager of the theatre had the idea of placing four wings of a windmill against the outside wall of the theatre, and illuminating them with red lamps. The lights and signs of Coney Island were no doubt in his mind. For very little extra money it was found that the wings could be made to revolve. This was the first moving sign in lights to appear on Broadway.

Victor Herbert was over fifty when he arrived at the pinnacle of his career both in light and serious music. The best of all his operettas, *Naughty Marietta,* was produced not long before his grand opera *Natoma* was sung in the Metropolitan Opera House in Philadelphia. In *Natoma* the composer was supposed to have made use of Indian themes. There was still a prejudice against American opera. Ever since Americans thought about opera at all, there had been the feeling in the United States that no music could be good if it had not come from Europe. People had got in the habit of hearing grand opera in foreign languages. Many of them thought, as no doubt there are some still who think, that an opera sung in English sounds silly. Habits of thinking change very, very slowly. It required a long time for Americans to be even tolerant of their own composers and musicians.

In time, the light operas turned out by "America's favorite composer" failed to draw. His popularity was on the wane. The fashion in show music was changing. Victor Herbert then wrote special numbers for the musical revues. When a producer tried to interpolate jazz pieces into the scores, Herbert would have none of it. He belonged to the days when the operetta was based on a romantic story; when it contained choral singing and ballads with a substantial orchestral accompaniment. These days were fast receding into the past. The popular musical show coming into fashion was the revue, or musical comedies in the revue style. The music was "jazzed." Herbert and the operetta were becoming "old stuff." There is nothing more out-of-date than the recent past. When people asked the composer why he didn't write another *Kiss Me Again* waltz, he would answer that he had written waltzes just as good, but that the public had changed; they didn't recognize them.

Victor Herbert's *Suite of Serenades* was played at the famous Whiteman concert for which Gershwin wrote the *Rhapsody in Blue.* He did not write jazz, but it was his first experience in writing for a jazz orchestra, and he complained a bit "about the doubling which he said hampered him." When he wanted an oboe, for instance, it disturbed him to find that the oboe player was busy with the bass clarinet.

Herbert generously offered to teach orchestration, in which he was a master, to George Gershwin. But not long after, Herbert died. He also tried to interest Irving Berlin in musical theory. He said to Berlin:

"It is a mistaken idea that a little science will hurt your natural flow of melody. On the contrary, a musical education will give you a background that will improve your work."

Herbert was the first important American composer to write an original score for a movie production. He composed to the very last. When not writing music, he was up late at night rehearsing what he had written. One May day after a late rehearsal, he stepped into one of his favorite restaurants for lunch. He passed the time of day with some friends, for he found friends everywhere. As he passed one who was lunching on wheat-cakes, he stopped and laughingly admonished him, saying that they were both getting too old to eat wheat-cakes. Soon afterward, the friend passed Herbert's table, and seeing him eating a sandwich, advised him to let it alone. But Herbert said:

"Charlie, I can eat nails."

Apparently he had always thought so, for one who knew him said that Herbert really ate himself to death.

At any rate, the sandwich was his last meal, for that afternoon he didn't feel well and went to see his doctor. The doctor was out, and before he came back, the musician had collapsed.

Deems Taylor wrote of Herbert, "He was the last of the troubadours . . . he had the gift of song. His music bubbled and sparkled and charmed and he brought gaiety to an art that often suffers from the pretentiousness and self-consciousness of its practitioners."

Victor Herbert, born in Dublin, Ireland, February 1, 1859. Died in New York City, May 27, 1924.

EDWARD MACDOWELL

"The only thing is to be as useful as we can."

The first white people came to this country in order to be free in the observance of their religion, which was so much a part of their lives. They and their descendants ought to have understood that other people, even their children, might wish for the same freedom in deciding questions for themselves. But the world is a long time a-learning. People still think, for the most part, that their own ways are the only right ways, and they want everybody else to do the same as they do. Sometimes there will be a man, however, who having been denied his dearest wishes in his own boyhood, will see that his son gets what he wants; a generous man who wants his son to have the opportunities he himself has missed.

While Abraham Lincoln was President of the United States, there lived in the Quaker quarter of New York City, at number 220 Clinton Street, a business man named Thomas MacDowell. He was himself a devout Quaker of Irish and Scotch descent. If Thomas, as a boy, had been able to do what he wanted, instead of having to do what his stern father wanted, he would probably have become an artist. When he was young, he could draw and paint very well, and he was intensely interested in art. He loved the outdoors, and would have much preferred to spend his days painting landscapes. But his father was one of those people who held the queer opinion that any artistic endeavor was not a man's work. No, his son must go into business. Therefore Friend Thomas spent his life going to an office in the city, day after day.

He had married a young and beautiful girl of English descent who was not a Quaker. They had two sons. Walter, the eldest, was three when Edward Alexander was born.

When Thomas' boys were little, they had to go to Quaker meeting on Sundays and sit for hours on hard, high-backed benches, often in absolute silence. There was no sermon, no music, no singing. Everything was silent unless the Spirit moved some Quaker to speak. The women sat on one side of the meeting-house and the men on the other. They were stiff services for young boys. These silent meetings made such a deep impression on Edward that when he grew to be a man and went to church where there was fine music and a sermon, he instinctively sat near the door. He never lost the feeling that he might be caught—locked in the pew as in a trap, with no chance of escape.

Though Thomas saw that his sons were started in life as good Quakers, he was much more lenient with them than his own father had been with him. Through him and his stern Quaker father, perhaps something in the blood was passed on to Edward from the Scotch and Irish ancestors.

Some of the most beautiful folk-music in the world has come from Scotland and Ireland. The folk-tales and legends of old Ireland abound in references to elves, sprites and fairy-folk, in which the people thoroughly believed. In America, the Quaker boy, Edward MacDowell may have inherited some of this quality from his Irish and Scotch forebears. At any rate, he sincerely believed in the little people of the woods. He loved to pore over the fascinating tales and legends. City boy as he was, he preferred the country, where he could ramble in the woods, where he could be alone with the hidden, friendly sprites.

Edward must have also inherited his father's gift for drawing, for he spent much time sketching and he did it very well. When his mother gave him a sketch-book, his father made no objection, remembering what drawing had meant to him.

Edward's mother, though neither artistic nor musical, had great ambitions for him. She saw that Edward had a natural sense of fun. She perceived that in her Quaker household there was a boy whose tastes were of a kind which Quakers considered frivolous—such tastes as music, colors, fairy-tales and adventure; a boy whose training and instincts were a combination of opposites. He would require careful handling, she thought. A city boy and a Quaker who was full of day-dreams, with an imagination which allowed him to live in a world of make-believe, must surely be out of the common run.

He wasn't a sissy, either. He could smash his toys, and he did, one Christmas when he and Walter grew tired of playing with some mechanical ones that "went" by themselves. He could also pitch in and fight—a most un-Quaker-like proceeding. One day not long after the end of the Civil War, when patriotic feelings were running high, seven-year-old Edward chanced on a little foreigner in the street, an urchin who said insulting things about the Flag. Edward would not stand that. He fought the street boy, and his mother found them rolling in the gutter. Years later, when Edward was in his 'teens and studying in Germany, he was walking down the street with an American friend who looked American in a foreign land. Edward could understand German by that time, and in passing a pompous-looking German policeman he heard the man make a slighting remark about his friend. Instantly he flew at the offending official. He had to be restrained by friends, for he was not on home soil. These incidents show that Edward, though a shy and sensitive lad, was ready to demand fair play.

When the boys were very young, their parents took them up to Central Park for picnics, to give them a chance to run. In those days the streets were not paved as they are now. There were no taxis and busses. Instead of stores on Fifth Avenue, there were beautiful homes, and Central Park was almost like the country.

The Park was about three miles away from the Mac-Dowell home "down" on Clinton Street. Mr. Mac-Dowell used to order the family horse, Whitey, hitched up, and would himself drive his family through the dirt streets for the much-anticipated outing. Soldiers in dark-blue uniforms frequently marched through the streets. Clothes were very different then. The ladies wore hoop-skirts which switched and swung along on the promenade. Little girls wore pantalettes hanging down from under their frocks. Little boys wore tight jackets. Older men wore tall hats like Abraham Lincoln's, tight trousers, and lemon-colored gloves. Conveyances were pulled by horses. There were no skyscrapers, no great apartment houses. People seemed to have time to live in a more leisurely way when they had no buttons to push, no electric lights and no telephone.

Since there were no radios and no victrolas, there was more time and inclination to read or to do other things for one's own entertainment. Edward was a great reader when he had to be indoors and, in or out, he loved to make drawings in his sketchbook. They were very good, too. In this book there is one that he drew of himself at fourteen. It shows that he was looking forward to having a fine mustache.

As for music, about the first lesson the MacDowell boys had took place during a visit to Grandfather Mac-Dowell's farm. Cousin Charles MacDowell, about a year older than Walter, was there too. While they were waiting for breakfast one cold morning, Edward's mother stood the boys in a row in the dining-room and taught them:

"Tramp, tramp, tramp the boys are marching. . . ."

Everybody in the north was singing that war-song. The boys marched around the room, singing and clapping their hands. Edward, the youngest, about three, could both keep the best rhythm and sing the tune most surely. So marked was his talent from the beginning, that the family bought a piano that he might have lessons. His teacher, a gentleman from South America, was invited to live in the MacDowell home. Grandfather thought it was outrageous. He thought Edward should be learning, as he said, "some useful work." He classed all musicians in the same category as the hand-organ man with a monkey.

Such an attitude was neither American nor Quaker. It was an attitude inherited from older times in Europe. If you read about Rachmaninoff, or Sibelius, you will see that their grandparents felt the same way. It was a prejudice which came down from the time when musicians were classed as servants. Only princes could afford to have musicians in their courts. Even Haydn, one of the greatest musicians, had to wear servants' livery in the court of his patron, Prince Esterhazy. Against this condition Beethoven had fought. He once told his kind patron, Prince Lobkowitz, in quite strong language that he considered his own talents and achievements lifted

him to a place deserving of fully as much respect as if
he had come from a wealthy and aristocratic family. Beethoven's independent attitude did a great deal to lift the
musician's social status in Europe. On the other hand,
there are some writers and musicians who have seen the
good side in the old system of patronage. Victor Herbert was one who thought that lack of musical patronage
in the United States was the greatest factor in retarding
the growth of our music. Certainly it is true that since
our country developed to a point where there has been
enough wealth to encourage the practice of the art, our
music has leaped forward.

Edward MacDowell was no prodigy. He enjoyed
his lessons and caught his teacher's enthusiasm for
music, but he did not like to practice. He much preferred to make up pieces on the piano. He also liked
to make up stories and pictures. Sometimes, after the
teacher had been showing Edward how a piece should
be played, he discovered with chagrin that his pupil,
meantime, had been quietly drawing a picture of him in
the music-book.

Edward had some very definite ideas. He did not
like nicknames, and hated to be called Ed or Eddie. He
disliked being fussed over and kissed, and having to
attend dancing-school. Going at all must have been
Mrs. MacDowell's idea, because it was un-Quakerish
to go to a dancing-school. However, Edward did, and,
being very good-looking, with his dark hair, bright
blue eyes, fine complexion with pink cheeks, found him-

self more popular with the girls than he wished to be. With his good sense of rhythm he was naturally a good dancer, but he much preferred to play baseball.

A brilliant young lady pianist came from South America, and her concerts in New York were played to crowded houses. This was Teresa Carreño, one of the greatest of women pianists. She was about eighteen at the time, but she had been a prodigy, playing beautifully at the age of nine. Through Edward's South American teacher, Mr. Buitrago, introductions were made, and Carreño called at the MacDowell home. When Edward played for her, she offered to give him lessons. Since Mr. Buitrago was really a violinist instead of pianist, piano lessons with him had been somewhat irregular. Edward now studied with a great pianist. Carreño was a Spanish beauty with a vital, warm manner. She liked to show her feelings, and was most un-Quakerlike in expressing herself. When Edward, therefore, played in a manner to please her, she was wont to catch him up in an embrace and kiss him. He loathed it! Carreño soon discovered his feelings. Thereafter, when he had not practiced and consequently played badly, she did not scold him, but only threatened to kiss him. This made him work for all he was worth.

He went first to public school, and later to a private French school. It was while the family were living in East 19th street near Third Avenue that Edward won a prize. Not for music, not for drawing or French, but for something which startled his father almost out of his wits. One day the boys, including Cousin Charles, were upstairs, and Walter said:

"What do you think Eddie has done now, Charles?"

"I don't know. What?"

"Eddie is a great boy!" went on Walter, very proud of his younger brother. "Look at this!" He took out of the bureau drawer a small pearl-handled, silver-mounted revolver. Walter added:

"How would *you* like to win that in a shooting-match? Eddie did it!"

They went down in the back yard and Walter fastened a card up on the brick wall for a target. After Walter and Charles fired a few shots, they insisted upon seeing how good Eddie was.

When Edward had casually returned home with a revolver a few days before, his father sternly asked him where he got it. Edward replied that he had seen it hanging in a window of a shooting-gallery on Third Avenue as he passed by. There was a notice announcing that it was offered as a prize to the person who would make the best score that day. So he just stepped in and —won the prize.

His father couldn't believe it. He took Edward and the pistol and marched off immediately to the shooting-gallery. The owner greeted them, told Mr. Mac-Dowell that the boy had beaten all the other marksmen and had fairly won the revolver. He ended by congratulating the father upon having a son so talented. It was years later, after Edward had become a fine pianist and composer, before his father could feel proud to tell the story. At the time he was dismayed.

When Edward was twelve, his mother took him abroad. The boy wanted to go to Ireland, the home of the legends he liked so well; to Scotland, where his own ancestors had worn kilts; to England, whence his mother's people had come. Then of course he wanted to go to France to try out the French learned in school, and to Germany, to hear music.

It was a summer rich in experiences which Edward MacDowell never forgot. In after years, he wrote a set of tone poems for piano, called *Sea Pieces,* in which he remembered his first impressions of being *In Mid-Ocean,* and of *A Wandering Iceberg.* Most Americans, when crossing the ocean for the first time, give a passing thought to the early Pilgrims, and wonder what the great Atlantic seemed like to the passengers on the *Mayflower* who spent almost three months at sea. MacDowell did, too, when he composed *A.D. 1620.*

He saw, in Switzerland, the land of William Tell, the super-marksman. There was a steamer trip up the Rhine and the travelers saw the castles of the robber-barons of olden days. But there was one experience Edward did not care to remember for a long time. It happened in Paris.

One day while in the beautiful French city, he wanted some candy. He had heard about French confectionery, and he went out in the streets of Paris by himself to look for a candy shop. The shops looked

[129]

very different from the shops at home, and nowhere did he see any candy displayed in windows. Then, seeing the word *Confections* on a sign, he went into the small store and asked the young lady clerk for *confections*. There was no candy to be seen on the counters or shelves, but he thought it was just the French way of doing things. He was puzzled by the giggling and the sly glances of amusement among the girls waiting upon him. When they brought *des confections* to him for his inspection, what was his horror to find that what he hoped would be candy turned out to be silk and lace underclothes and dressing-gowns for ladies! It was a lesson in French that he never had to learn over again. He hurried out of that store, taking his red face with him.

When he was thirteen he finished at the French school in New York, and thereafter his study was all music. His mother was determined that he should become a great pianist. Three years after the sight-seeing trip to Europe, the two went over again. Edward was now fifteen. This time he was placed in the care of the Head of the French Conservatory in Paris for serious musical study. Working now in real earnest, he began at six in the morning and never stopped until nine at night, studying musical theory and composition besides piano. Also he had to perfect himself in the French language.

One day in a French lesson he was occupied with his sketching. Whenever he had a pencil in his hand he was always sketching. The teacher, noticing that his pupil was hiding something behind his French grammar, asked to see it. Edward expected a scolding surely, since he had very accurately drawn the teacher himself, doing full justice to the man's unusually big nose. To Edward's surprise, however, the teacher, after looking at the picture, asked where he had studied drawing. The boy had to admit that he had never studied drawing anywhere. The French master wondered how he could have acquired such skill and said he would keep the drawing.

The matter did not end there. Some days later, the French teacher called on Mrs. MacDowell and explained that he had a friend who was a great artist. He had shown the artist Edward's sketch, for he was much impressed to see how truly Edward had portrayed him. The artist had made an astounding proposal. Not only would he teach Edward free for three years, but he would also support him, so that living and food need cost the MacDowells nothing. He held out bright hopes that Edward would become a great painter.

It was an alluring temptation. The music study in Europe was costing the MacDowells a great deal of money. They had had to do considerable figuring in the matter of expenses to be able to send the boy away at all. Now suddenly the opportunity was presented to Edward of receiving as a gift, pure and simple, the chance of perfecting himself in another art, for which he also had a talent. Painter or pianist, which should he be? He had already worked very hard at music; and the drawing was fun. He loved to do both. The one pursuit would be expensive; the other, free. Either one would involve great labor, since it is impossible to become expert in anything without constant, hard, and loving work. Another composer, talented in both lines, had once been faced with the same choice. Charles Gounod, who had received the coveted Prix de Rome for composition, was also offered one for drawing. He remained faithful to his music, however. And so did MacDowell. His mother returned to America, and Edward lived in Paris with his first teacher, Mr. Buitrago, who had accompanied the Americans to Europe.

Edward spent one vacation with a French friend on a farm near Chartres. It was a wonderful experience to live with a French family. When the organist at the village church discovered that a musician was staying nearby, he asked the visitor to substitute for him, while he went away on a vacation. Young Mac-Dowell played the organ in a church where the services were a great contrast to the Quaker meetings of his childhood.

After two years of study in Paris, he became restless. He had transposed most of the Bach preludes and fugues into other keys, which was excellent musical discipline, but he felt that his piano-playing was not advancing as rapidly as it should. He wanted to make a change. He knew that he had acquired a solid musi-

cal foundation in Paris, but after hearing the great
Rubinstein play, he felt that in France he could never
learn to play like that. He wanted to work with a brilliant pianist. A year went by while he studied in the
beautiful little German city of Wiesbaden; then he went
to the Conservatory at Frankfort. There he studied
composition with Raff, some of whose pieces are still
played by pupils in piano. His teachers were sympathetic and encouraging. At the end of two years Mac-
Dowell's playing had become brilliant, and his piano
teacher, Heymann, recommended him to teach in his
place when he became ill. But not all the German professors were sympathetic. There are always some "old
fogey" musicians, both young and old, who cannot instil
life into their music no matter how hard they try. Some
of them even think that just playing notes is enough.
They have no touch with the human side of art or of life,
and all they think of is correctness, notes, rules, muscles,
hand positions, and that kind of thing. That is important, of course. But notes, even though they are scales,
or arpeggios, or Czerny, can and should be played with
life and a dash of good red blood. They live then.
The notes are what Sibelius would call "alive." Scales
and arpeggios become rewarding to the player, and
Czerny and Clementi can be great fun. Some of these
professors did not approve of MacDowell's fresh and
vivid manner of playing, and they would not permit him
to teach in Heymann's place. But Raff sent him some

pupils, privately, and MacDowell did begin to teach in Germany.

At this time he was known as the "handsome American," for his fine physique, fair skin with keen, blue eyes, reddish mustache and jet-black hair.

One summer day when he was nineteen, who should turn up in Frankfort but Cousin Charles, riding on a high bicycle. The two boys had not seen each other for years. Edward made his cousin comfortable in his agreeable apartments, and Charles was as much impressed by Edward's easy manner of living and working in a foreign country as he had been when little Edward won the revolver for straight shooting.

Among the pupils whom the kindly Raff sent to his favorite American was Miss Marian Nevins of Connecticut. Raff was of the opinion that a girl from the United States would do better with a teacher who knew her language, though she was rather averse to having an American for a teacher when she had gone all the way to Europe for study. She consented, however, to study with MacDowell for a year. He, on his part, also preferred to have European students, for the experience. For the first year he gave her Bach and études with never a "piece," and even after such severe training, she declined a chance to study with Clara Schumann to remain a pupil of MacDowell.

It was Raff who first encouraged the "handsome American" to compose. When he heard Edward's *First Piano Concerto*, he told him it was good enough to play to Liszt. Rare praise, indeed! Raff gave MacDowell a letter of introduction to Liszt, and one day the American screwed up his courage enough to go to Weimar, where Liszt lived. But after he came to the great pianist's house, he sat down on a bench outside the door, afraid to enter. After a time he went inside, but again sat down in the vestibule. Some of the pupils, going in to one of Liszt's famous class lessons, must have told the master about the scared young man waiting near the door clutching music paper in his hand. Liszt came out into the hall, and MacDowell knew instantly that the distinguished-looking gentleman was the great artist he had come to see. Presenting his letter, he was graciously invited to come in and play his composition. Even though he was too shy in this new and wonderful surrounding, too deeply awed by playing for Liszt and his pupils, to do his best, the great man praised him not only for his concerto, but for his playing. Liszt did even more for him than give him praise. It was he who was influential in helping MacDowell have his compositions played in Germany.

The good teacher, Raff, was gratified to learn that MacDowell's *First Piano Suite* was to be played by a German Society of Musicians, at the word of Liszt. He was looking forward to the day; but alas, a blow fell. Just before the event was to take place, Raff died. MacDowell was crushed, for he deeply loved his kind and understanding teacher. In need of sympathy he called upon his own American pupil, Miss Nevins, who advised him to work even harder. Two weeks later he played his suite at the concert, and was surprised that it should be received with cries of "Bravo." He was so modest that it was the first time he ever thought that anyone else might enjoy music of his own writing. This spurred him on, and when Liszt recommended his first works for publication in Germany, he dedicated his concerto to Liszt. He worked hard, writing, practicing, teaching, and—he fell in love with his American pupil, Miss Nevins.

The summer he was twenty-three, MacDowell came to America for a month and was married in Connecticut. The newly-married pair returned to Europe, where they traveled for some weeks before taking up their abode in Germany.

MacDowell taught for several more years there, and by the time he returned to his native country to live, he had spent almost as many years in Europe as he had in the United States.

The MacDowells then lived in Boston. The composer had many successes. The triumph he most cherished was the evening when he played his *Second Concerto* with the Boston Symphony Orchestra and they also played his *Indian Suite*. That evening he was presented with a laurel wreath, which he always kept hanging on the wall in his New Hampshire farm. Though he was deeply pleased when his work was appreciated, MacDowell was shy and embarrassed when being praised. He hated and feared insincerity. He showed his appreciation to his parents by paying back to them all the money they had spent for his musical education.

While he lived in Boston, he had two dogs of whom he was very fond: a collie named Charlemagne, and later a little terrier named Charlie. Charlie was the composer's constant companion on the farm where the MacDowells spent their summers. Charlie became a music critic, for he was taught to bark happily when he heard the music of Wagner, but to howl dismally when he heard Brahms!

Being invited to become Professor of Music at Columbia University, MacDowell returned again to his native city to live. By that time, the house in Clinton Street, where he had spent his boyhood, was gone. In its place stood an ugly tenement house, for that section had become part of the East Side. Immigrants swarmed there, people who had come to America looking for an easier living. It was just about this time that one family of immigrants, named Baline, came from Russia, and the four-year-old Baline boy grew up to be the popular song-writer, Irving Berlin, composer of *Alexander's Ragtime Band* and *God Bless America*.

MacDowell gave of his best to his teaching at Columbia and to building up a music department. He was very generous to pupils who showed ability and a strong will to work, and to many of these who had no money he gave free lessons. He had a delightful sense of humor, and an infectious laugh. Once when a pupil had filled up empty spaces in an exercise-book with a series of rests and placed a double-bar at the end, Mac-Dowell returned the book with a red line marked around the rests, having written in the margin: "This is the only correct passage in the exercise."

Just before a recital he would be in a constant turmoil of alternating eagerness and doubts, a combination of restless anticipation and stage-fright. His wife would usually give him his final push into his program. After he gave so much time to teaching, it was his playing which suffered most, and although he could play so well that a New York critic had once written of him that he was the most satisfying pianist he had heard since Paderewski, MacDowell was wretched if he felt that he had played badly.

He loved to get away from the city, and to tramp over New Hampshire hills and go riding in a sulky with his farmer. He did most of his composing when he could get completely away from everyday interferences, and for this he had a little cabin in the woods on his farm in Peterboro, New Hampshire. The little cabin is still there. But the farm is now a colony for artists, writers, composers, and such people whose work is done better when they do not have to think of answering telephones, ordering lunch, and the dozens of disturbances that crop up throughout the day. After MacDowell died, Mrs. MacDowell contributed her time and energy to give other artists what her husband used to wish for—solitude in which to think and write. Now there are twenty cabins hidden away among the MacDowell woods, and many American composers have enjoyed a sojourn there.

From his boyhood days, MacDowell always loved to read. Someone wrote of him that he had "intellectual interests and broad culture in great contrast to the brainlessness of the average musician." That he had varied and wide tastes is shown in his many hobbies. Though he was a great reader of poetry, and knew a good deal about legendary lore and medieval romance, he loved to read Mark Twain and the Uncle Remus stories. Gardening, photography and carpentry were also his delight. He even planned gardens and designed buildings. Once he skipped away from attending a faculty meeting in order to go to a prize-fight! He was happy to discover that about a third of his colleagues had done the same thing.

When he learned that the little village of Peterboro had no golf-course, he bought a farm, presented it to the village, induced a generous neighbor to build a clubhouse, and invited everyone—even the poorest—to come and enjoy the "royal game."

No matter how busy he was with teaching, he always felt that it was necessary to write at least a few bars of music every day. His early discipline in France convinced him that it was as important to have daily practice in writing as it was to have daily practice on the piano. He never composed at the piano, but often, when improvising, he would have ideas which he wrote

[139]

down in a sketchbook. Later on, sometimes at the farm in summertime, he could refer to his notes and use these ideas for themes. Of his four big piano sonatas, he felt the most satisfaction with the *Keltic Sonata*. He considered it the most complete and best constructed of all his larger works. He dedicated it, as well as his *Norse Sonata*, to Grieg, of whose music he was very fond. Of his smaller works, he liked the *Sea Pieces* best as a whole, but he loved the *Dirge* from the *Indian Suite*.

When the Bohemian composer, Dvořák, was in this country and wrote his *New World Symphony*, Mac-Dowell did not feel that his method of using Negro melodies was the way to make an "American" music. He did not think that a style that could be called American was going to be so easily found. Although he himself used Indian melodies, he never regarded the music as "American" for that reason. Elgar felt somewhat the same, for he would never consciously use folk-tunes. MacDowell said:

"A man is generally something different from the clothes he wears or the business he is occupied with; but when we do see a man identified with his clothes we think but little of him. And so it is with music. So-called Russian, Bohemian, or any other purely national-istic music has no place in art, for its characteristics may be duplicated by anyone who takes the fancy to do so. On the other hand, the vital element of music—personality—stands alone. Music that can be made by 'recipe' is not music, but 'tailoring.' Such means of making a national music is childish. Before a people can find a musical writer to echo its genius it must first possess men who truly represent it—that is to say, men who, being part of the people, love the country for itself: men who put into their music what the nation has put into its life; and in the case of America it needs, above all, both on the part of the public and on the part of the writer, absolute freedom from the restraint that an almost unlimited deference to European thought and prejudice has imposed upon us. Masquerading in the so-called nationalism of Negro clothes cut in Bohemia will not help us. What we must arrive at is the youthful optimistic vitality and the undaunted tenacity of spirit that characterizes the American man."

Our first American-born composer of serious music to be known and published in Europe has now been dead for over forty years, but as you read through these stories of other composers' lives and work, perhaps you will feel that MacDowell's ideas on American music ring true. Though it takes longer than a man's lifetime for an art to mature, perhaps you may feel that, at last, what MacDowell called "youthful optimistic vitality and the undaunted tenacity of spirit" is creeping into the music which Americans are writing.

Edward MacDowell, born in New York City, December 18, 1861. Died there, January 23, 1908.

ETHELBERT NEVIN

"Bach is my daily bread."

When Stephen Foster died there was a little boy a year and a half old, named Ethelbert Nevin, growing up in the same part of the country where Foster had spent his childhood. It was in the vicinity of Pittsburgh, Pennsylvania. When Foster was little, Pittsburgh was a river town still very near to pioneer ways, and the wild frontier lay just beyond to the west. The fascinating steamboating life on the river brought him in contact with the songs of the Negro roustabouts. He heard the music of lowly people entertaining each other. Ethelbert Nevin became a song-writer, too, but there was nothing about his songs to remind one of Foster. His whole life was very different. He had training in music which Foster missed, but both of them were late to start on their musical path, because in those days and in pioneer America, musical sons were strange fruit which parents did not understand how to cultivate. Foster's songs were directly from the heart and addressed to the heart. Nevin's songs were his impressions—poetic fancies about his subjects, the artificial rather than the natural, yet to him just as real and therefore treated sincerely.

When Nevin was growing up, Pittsburgh had become a railroad center. This brought the Eastern cities along the Atlantic nearer to the Middle West. The distance which Foster's parents had traveled on horseback for their honeymoon, which took two weeks to cover, could in Ethelbert Nevin's boyhood be traversed in a few hours by train. Stephen Foster never dreamed of going so far away as crossing the ocean, but Nevin made many trips to Europe. He studied there, and with the European tradition in music he felt most at home. His bringing up was more like that of Edward MacDowell, who was just a year older. But MacDowell lived in New York, and then went abroad in his middle 'teens, so the two never met until they were grown men, and full-fledged musicians—both composers and both pianists of considerable virtuosity. One who heard them both, said, "MacDowell plays more like the devil. Nevin plays like a poet."

The Nevins were, like the MacDowells and the Fosters, of Scotch-Irish ancestry. Ethelbert's father had known Pittsburgh as it was in Foster's day. He was very likely attending Jefferson College at the very time when Stephen Foster entered. But then Stephen left again before a week was out. Later, Mr. Nevin wrote an article on Stephen Foster and Negro minstrelsy. Ethelbert's mother was a lady of refinement and culture. When she was a girl, it was for her that a grand piano was carted by horses across the Allegheny Mountains from the east. She was very fond of music.

The Nevin homestead, called "Vineacre," where

Nevin was born, was in Edgeworth, near Sewickley on the Ohio River about fifteen miles south of Pittsburgh. It was a large, rambling house which was just the kind to endear itself to children who played in it. And there were many to play, for the Nevins had eight children, of whom Ethelbert was the fifth.

As he was born while the Civil War was in progress, he heard the songs which were then so popular from the time he was in the cradle. At three he could sing *Tenting on the Old Camp Ground* and *Marching Through Georgia*. When he was five he could accompany himself on the piano while he sang. He was eager, even then, to learn about music. When he saw his older cousins starting off to their music lessons, he would roll up some music, tuck it under his arm and try to leave the house. Being questioned as to where he was going, he would reply, "Oh, I must go and take my music lessons." The night before Christmas of that same year, his father came home with a music-box in his pocket. He took the little fellow on his knee and told him the story of the first Christmas time. Occasionally, to make the story more effective, he would reach in his pocket, touch off the spring of the music-box, and the sweet little tinkle of sounds filled the air. The boy became intensely excited, and firmly believed that the musical sounds came from the angels in heaven.

Ethelbert never enjoyed boys' sports and games; he much preferred playing with girls. However, he was greatly elated when the boys made him the water-carrier for the baseball team. He felt it to be an honor. It was perhaps just as well. Frequently it happened that when he did join in a ball game, there would be a moment when he would drop his bat on the ground, suddenly rush into the house and go to the piano. When asked why he did this, he replied, "Because I just thought of something I wanted to play."

At eight he had his first lessons on the piano with a teacher. From early childhood he had a nervous, high-strung temperament which was not helped by his being "shown-off" by his colored nurse and constantly asked to sing his little pieces or to dance. Not long after his lessons began, he also commenced to write his own melodies. His first composition was written for his younger sister, and named for her, the *Lillian Polka*. On the cover he had printed:

> *By Bertie Nevin*
> *Aged eleven.*

His first school was in Edgeworth, where the rector of the Episcopal Church was also the schoolmaster, and school was held in church. Many of the students were Nevin cousins of Bertie's, in fact there were so many Nevins in the town that the community joke was that the churchgoers sometimes became confused in their prayers, and said, "Our father which art a Nevin."

Bertie had a clear, sweet soprano voice, and sang in the concerts given by the Nevin Octette and the Gounod Club. The year of his first composition, he also played in his first public concert, the Wagner-Liszt *Tannhäuser March*.

When he was fifteen, his parents took him and his sister Lillie on a trip to Europe. Bertie was given the opportunity to study music in Dresden, and to hear the finest music in Leipzig, Berlin and Vienna. They paid a visit to Rome, where a cousin Nevin was rector in the Episcopal Church, and Bertie sang in the choir. He probably sang too much at that time when his voice was changing, because later on, his singing voice was never strong, which was a disappointment to him. In the autumn, after the Nevins returned to Vineacre, Bertie entered the Freshman class of what is now the University of Pittsburgh.

But he was not a college type. He was companionable enough with his own friends, but he was not the hail-fellow-well-met with everybody. Nor was he keen on academic studies; he much preferred to study by his own reading and, later on, by his many travels. During his year at college—for his Freshman year was also his last year—music was still his first interest. He played the Chopin *E flat Polonaise* with the Pittsburgh orchestra, and he also took part in a performance by the Sewickley Minstrels. That year he wrote songs which were later published.

When he brought up the idea of wanting to become a professional musician, there was trouble with his father. It was the same story which you have come across many times if you have read other stories about composers. Mr. Nevin thought music was all right as an accomplishment, but to make a business of it, no! There was no money in it. Musicians and actors he lumped together as being not quite their kind of people. Anyway, Bertie would probably starve if he tried to live on music. With these strong arguments, Father won; and Bertie tried to be a business man.

For a time he worked in the printing establishment in which two of his older brothers were interested. In front of the shop there was a large store-window, and the Sewickley girls would come and linger in front of the window, when on their shopping errands in town, and watch Bertie at work. But even with these attentions he could not become interested in the business. He had no aptitude for it when he was always thinking of the music he wanted to be doing. One night he went to his father, who was sitting in his library at home, and said:

"Let me be poor all my life and be a musician."

Perhaps Bertie's mother had been quietly taking his side in the family discussions as to his future. At any rate, his father at last consented, and at eighteen Bertie began to work in the way he should have done many years earlier.

In a small place like Vineacre he had to rely on a correspondence course for study in musical theory. He did this by letters exchanged with an English musician who was teaching in New York. It was this year when his second composition appeared, a lively song called *Apple-Blossom.* He did not sign his own name to this piece, but used his middle name, Woodbridge, as a *nom de plume.*

There were many social affairs, and Bertie was not averse to joining in the fun. The girls he had grown up with were now away at boarding-school, but some of them were no further away than Pittsburgh— near enough to return frequently for week-ends. In the spring, one of the girls brought two of her friends home for a holiday, and they were met at the station by Bertie Nevin and two other boys.

In those days when there were no automobiles; country walks and rambles were the thing. One of the boys knew where there was a grapevine swing; they might go try that. The girls thought, too, that it might be fun, and they crossed the river and went up a hill until they came to the swing. It was immense. The ropes were so long that it could swing way across a little valley. The gallant boys tried the swing first to make sure it was safe for the girls. Then Bertie and Billie Woods thought it might be a good thing to get on the swing together and "work up." They climbed on, stood facing each other, and coaxed the swing higher and higher. It was glorious. Out over the valley they soared, while the admiring girls and the other boy watched and waved from below, shouting and laughing.

Suddenly the rope broke. The two passengers dropped like plummets into the little valley below. Bertie arrived first, with Billie landing on top of him.

[148]

The Sewickley girl who was hostess of the week-end was really frightened; but her beautiful friend, Anne Paul, was so overcome by the funny expression on Bertie's face as he went sailing through the air, that she shook with laughter. The only casualty was Bertie's sprained ankle. For that reason the party in the evening was held at Vineacre. All Bertie could contribute was the playing for the dancing. But he remarked to others that although Anne Paul was no doubt very beautiful, she was certainly the coldest girl he had ever met. Her laughter at his fall was still rankling in the young pianist's mind.

Six months later Bertie was invited to a New Year's Eve party at Anne Paul's home on the other side of Pittsburgh. Her father provided a special train to bring his daughter's guests. Bertie Nevin, the strange boy who liked music and flowers, a sensitive, nervous sort of chap, was very different from the college boys whom Anne knew. She herself was almost a tomboy. She loved horseback riding and outdoor life. Strange that she should have remembered a boy like Bert. Not only that, but when she looked over her guests in choosing her partner with whom to dance the final German, it was Bertie to whom she impulsively gave her tinseled favor.

The rest of the spring and summer, Ethelbert continued his correspondence course, and played the organ in church. In the autumn it was decided that he should have more serious education in music. Boston was at that time the center for music and composers; so to Boston Bertie went. While he was there, Anne finished her studies and was sent abroad with a group of girls to have her education rounded out with the stamp of foreign travel.

Serious work at last began for Ethelbert Nevin. He was given a thorough grounding in scales, exercises and Cramer studies. His teacher in piano had been a pupil of Liszt, and he required Nevin to practice one scale alone, with special fingering, for an hour and a half every day. He wrote to his mother that the exercises he had been given in Dresden some years before were Paradise compared to what he had to do now. When he had at last a teacher in composition, it was the same thing. He was drilled in the fundamentals which he should have begun to study at least eight years earlier. How much time had been lost in the process of getting his father to change his mind! It made these years infinitely harder for Ethelbert Nevin. He should have had these drills when his ardor was fresh, and not after his hopes had been deferred and his mind taken on a yearning which had gone so long unfulfilled. As a result, his moods were alternating ones of enthusiastic happiness in his work, and periods of depressing doubts when he wondered if he could ever attain the goal which seemed so far away. Also after spending so many years at home, he was now subject to spells of homesickness. His mother was ever very close to him, and her sympathy bound him to her in a way more closely than one finds in most boys. He used to write her that he simply *had* to find twenty-five hours in the day, or else he could never do the work which his teachers expected of him. More than once he strained his hand by constant practice. Nothing daunted, he would write her that he "did not want to stop for anything."

There was a second year in Boston, during which Ethelbert tried to get pupils as well as a position as organist in order to help pay his expenses. But he found neither, and his moods continued to swing from elation to deep discouragement. He thought of himself at this time more as a pianist than as a composer. He wrote, "Oh, how discouraged and tired I am of this continual practice, practice, practice, from morning to night; and think how many years it will be before I am able to play in an artistic manner." Yet in the same letter he told his mother that his teacher had complimented him for his good playing on a public program. As to his composing, he said at that time, "My brain is full of ideas," though he felt that he needed to learn better how to set them down on music-paper.

Then came a winter at home when Nevin rented a studio in Pittsburgh and announced himself as a teacher and pianist. Two more songs were published that year, *I Once Had a Sweet Little Doll, Dears,* and *When All the World is Young, Lad.* During this winter he and the girl who had laughed when he fell off the swing, fell in love with each other. After they became engaged, Nevin sailed for Europe the summer that he was twenty-one. Strange to say, it was Anne's father, a business man, who seemed to understand Nevin's need for music and study better than his own father.

He wrote his older brothers, who were giving him the money for his year abroad, that he was fascinated by Berlin. It was there he lived and worked. His teacher was Klindworth, whom he did not like at first, considering him a tyrant; but later he came to regard him as the one who had taught him the most, and they became the closest of friends. Even in the midst of such a wonderful year of opportunity—hearing music in Germany, studying without interruptions, and learning German—he wrote that at times it seemed a hopeless task, and that he would hardly advise anyone to become a professional musician.

There were parties and operas, it was not all work. Nevin's social life in Berlin was quite gay. He attended balls and concerts. His teacher took him to the opera in his own box, which was next to the king's, and Ethelbert wrote home that during the intermissions their box "was the center of Dukes, Counts, Countesses—more than I have ever seen together."

He was fortunate enough to stretch the year into two; for he went home the following summer on a visit and returned for a second year of study in Berlin. On the way, he stopped over in London and saw a performance of *The Mikado* by Gilbert and Sullivan, and he thought it was "positively fascinating." The second year must have been quite perfect for him, since Anne and her sister went over, too. The Christmas party that year was one of the real, gay, old-time festivals of singing and dancing among friends for which the old Germany was famous. Nevin did not know how fortunate he was to be there under the mistletoe, hearing and singing *O Tannenbaum,* and *Stille Nacht.* For later, music was killed for a time in the land that had been specially blessed with it. War and music do not thrive together; when a nation's thoughts are on war, music steals away.

In warmer days of spring there were picnics, river-trips, and visits to old Heidelberg, so that there were times when Nevin did not have to sit in front of the keyboard. If you read the whole book on the story of Nevin's life, you will find delightful descriptions of a student's life of those times in Germany.

When he returned to America, he made his début as a pianist in Pittsburgh, with brilliant success. Then followed years of playing in concerts and of composing. When he was twenty-six, he and Anne were married. They made their home in Massachusetts, either in Boston or in the vicinity. At times, he did some teaching. He wrote many songs and pieces for piano.

There were other visits to Europe. He was there when his piano pieces, *Water Scenes,* were published. Among these was the *Narcissus* which became so popular that it was played and thrummed around the world. It was a tune which became a fad. Hundreds of thousands of copies were sold. It was played by orchestras, organs, and hurdy-gurdies. The Prince of Wales commanded a performance of it. It was played on mouthorgans by Klondike miners, and every piano pupil wanted to learn it. Thereafter, the poor composer got no rest from it. Every time he played in public, he was forced to play as an encore what he began to call "that nasty little *Narcissus*."

After he had two children, a boy and a girl, he was once looking for an apartment in Paris where the family could live for a time. The one he liked the best was an apartment over one occupied by Rosa Bonheur, the painter of *The Horse Fair*. But the Nevins could not live there, for the artist objected to having a piano in the apartment overhead, and Nevin wrote that "an apartment with Michael Angelo and Shakespeare in the same building wouldn't do me much good if I could not use a piano."

When he lived in America, Nevin gave concerts and composed most of the time. In Boston, he knew MacDowell, and they played on a program together, but neither of them belonged to any group of musicians. MacDowell was too shy and reserved to care for it; and the weighty Boston musicians rather looked down their noses at Nevin, considering him a light-weight musically. But MacDowell was artist enough to appreciate Nevin's place, musically, and he realized that though Nevin was no composer of symphonies, he was capable of inventing melodies that were fresh and spontaneous.

He once said that the lilting strains of *Narcissus* would live long after many "labored, manufactured symphonies were forgotten."

Nevin was never very strong. He felt it necessary at times to live in the quiet of the old world to ease his high-strung nerves. European life was sympathetic to him; he enjoyed studying there and working in a way which was not possible for him in America, where his time was spent on concertizing and money-earning. With his family he lived in Italy for a while during his last visit to Europe, and there, one Christmas Eve, his wife heard him play a ghostly concert to his music dream-children. After he had begun to play, she slipped into the room. He did not know she was there. He was playing very softly, and singing, "Everywhere, Everywhere, Christmas Tonight." Then he "wandered off into strange improvisations. He played things more wonderful than he ever played before or after. And while he played, all the dream-children of his beautiful songs came and gathered round him in the shadowy room. He seemed to *see* them all. . . . He spoke to them in a confidential voice, saying: 'This is for you, Little Boy Blue'; and then turning to where Wynken and Blynken and Nod stood together, he would say: 'And now this is for you—just for you three alone.' . . . One after the other all the children of his songs came to him —the little girl whose doll was broken, and the little boy who got up at night—and each of them he welcomed with smiles and gentle words." Later on, his doctor said

[155]

that these extraordinary fancies "which could have occurred only in a poet's brain" might be attributed to the
effects of influenza.

Ethelbert Nevin composed music which had grace
and charm, appealing to people of his time. His melodies were tuneful. He was not a great composer, nor
did he attempt the greater music-forms. The sentiment
of his music, though obvious, was nevertheless sincere.
To read the story of his life; to listen to his kind of
music; and then to read the life of Irving Berlin, makes
it seem incredible that Nevin was the composer of the
song, which of all the songs in the world, Berlin once
wished he might have written. That song is *The Rosary*.

Nevin was thirty-five when he wrote *The Rosary*.
He was living in New York at the time. He received
a letter from his mother one day, in which she enclosed
a clipping from a newspaper. It was the poem, *The
Rosary*, by Robert Cameron Rogers. A friend had cut
it out of the newspaper and given it to her some years
before. Nevin had it a month before he did anything
with it. Then one day he picked it up, read it over
memorizing the words, and in a single sitting sketched
the song. He took it to his wife for a present, and gave
it to her with the note.

> Just a little souvenir to let you know I thank the *bon
> Dieu* for giving me you. The entire love and devotion of
> Ethelbert Nevin.

Such sweetness and spontaneous expressions of his
liking for certain people was a characteristic of Nevin

which went all through his life. Even as a child he would suddenly appear in front of his mother or a sister with a bouquet of flowers.

The Rosary is the song which has sold more copies than any other song in the world. It was a song, which in the language of Tin Pan Alley needed no plugging; it was a "natural."

One writer thinks that if Nevin had written nothing else, he would be always remembered for his song *Little Boy Blue.* His wife said that it had been written on the backs of several envelopes during a railway journey. He wrote other children's songs, and he was commissioned to write one for the Chicago World's Fair. He set German and French poems to music, and wrote some Christmas carols. Another song *Mighty Lak' a Rose,* was published after he died, and it also became so popular that it sold by the thousands.

On Valentine's Day, the last year of Nevin's life, when he lived in New Haven, Connecticut, he arranged a party for his little girl. His boy was away at school. His wife was absent at the time, so he decorated the apartment with ribbons and flowers, and sent carriages for the little guests he had invited to his daughter's party. He entertained them, played for dances, romped in the games, and sang them songs about children. When a neighbor looked in, he laughed and said, "I'm having the time of my life!"

It was his last party, for three days afterward he

died. During his lifetime, his songs did not bring him enough money to pay his living-expenses. Afterwards, *The Rosary* alone made a fortune.

Ethelbert Nevin, born at "Vineacre" near Pittsburgh, Pennsylvania, November 26, 1862. Died in New Haven, Connecticut, February 17, 1901.

Interlude

CHANGING FASHIONS IN POPULAR MUSIC

"A change to a new type of music is something to beware of as a hazard of all our fortunes. For the modes of music are never disturbed without unsettling of the most fundamental political and social conventions. . . ."

—PLATO

Since the times of the ancient bards, happenings of the day, events of history, deeds of heroes, have been told in songs and ballads. All nations have their ballads and popular songs, but it was in the new country of the United States where a new way of living was forged under new political ideas that the most startling changes took place in popular music.

We have seen that the spirituals were the result of giving religious songs to the Negro on the Southern plantations, and that the songs of the minstrel shows were the result of the impressions upon the white man of the colored man's music. Following the spirituals came another type of Negro music which came to be called the "blues." From the minstrel show, songs and sentimental ballads, evolved a new dance time which was called ragtime.

[159]

It was during the most important years in the development of popular music in the United States, that the composer Brahms, living in central Europe, became interested in American ragtime and wrote to a friend that he was thinking of making use of it himself. Not many years after this, however, he died. For some time during these years the Bohemian composer, Dvořák, lived in the United States and became greatly interested in Negro music. It was during these years that several of the American composers were either growing up, or were just being born.

Someone once said of the new ragtime: "There is a swing about it that holds even the most cultivated ear." This "swing" was to be stressed and developed more and more. The Negroid rhythms had insinuated into the popular music a new tempo, and a nervous rhythm insistent with its haltings and pushings of syncopation. Syncopation itself was not new. The gypsy music, Hungarian songs and dances, as well as the music of old Spain were full of it. But the ragtime syncopation was one of different flavor.

Ragtime became a fad. Then, by an easy step, playing ragtime came to be considered an accomplishment. Lessons could be had cheaply. It came to be the thing for people to have their own pianos. The growing popularity of ragtime in the 1890's was the impetus which spread a proficiency in instrumental playing throughout the country. Ragtime was just the right music for a people who were going dance-crazy. When people had instruments it was easier to sell music to them, and from this developed the great national industry of Tin Pan Alley.

On 28th street in New York, in the short block between Sixth Avenue and Broadway, clustered the offices of the publishers of popular music. In these offices were little rooms with almost no furnishing except for the little "tin pan" piano. There were dozens of them within the block, where a hammering and pounding of pianos went on from morning till night. This was the section called Tin Pan Alley. Its slogan was "anything to sell a song." Since those early days, Tin Pan Alley has moved up—both uptown in New York, and also upward in the quality of its "parlors." In Irving Berlin's boyhood days, he used to scramble up a narrow stairway to one of these dingy rooms to pound out, with one finger, a tune which was running in his head. George Gershwin was a plugger in Tin Pan Alley. Nowadays, Mr. Berlin's offices, where popular songs are still being published, are spacious. Rugs and pictures adorn the rooms. Tin Pan Alley is gradually putting on a more polite aspect.

During and after World War I, ragtime became jazz, and another style danced into popularity. In time the proficiency in instrumental playing produced a style of jazz called "swing music," in which the instrumentalists improvised variations upon a theme, or improvised accompanying melodies—a kind of popular counterpoint.

[161]

The Ragtime Instructor, which appeared in the early days of ragtime, was written by Ben Harney, a pioneer ragtime composer and pianist from Louisville who became a fad in New York. He created great excitement by "ragging the scale" in his performances. He also "ragged" Mendelssohn's *Spring Song* and Rubinstein's *Melody in F.* He was thus also a pioneer musician of a type that was to become very necessary to Tin Pan Alley—the arranger.

Irving Berlin, for instance, picked out his songs with one finger, because he simply did not know how to play. But there were plenty of people who could play with all ten fingers and who knew how to write music down on paper, who could never have thought up a tune. These were the arrangers. They would say to a songster, "Hum your tune." Then they wrote it down, supplying the harmonies and the accompaniment. From setting a simple tune to an harmonic accompaniment, or playing a classical melody to "ragged" harmonies and rhythms, the arrangers' duties grew to the making of arrangements for new combinations of instruments. The "blue" tones of the saxaphone,—an instrument whose use was encouraged by Handy, ushered in an era when dance orchestras dropped the violins of Victor Herbert's romantic style, and used, instead, the winds and percussions required by jazz.

Some song-writers write their own words; others write only the tunes, and there are men who supply the words. They are called lyricists. Ira Gershwin wrote many of the words for his brother's songs. George Gershwin wrote the *Rhapsody in Blue* for two pianos, and the arranger, Ferde Grofé, made the orchestral score which was equally necessary for its instant popularity. It was Ferde Grofé's grandfather, a cellist, who played at the same desk with Victor Herbert in the orchestra of the Metropolitan Opera House.

Tin Pan Alley supplied everything for its own particular type of music—the melodies, the words and the arrangements. But it lacked restraint. Constant ragging, jazzing, and "hotting-up" of melodies seemed to burn them up quickly. The less original of the jazz writers needed, it appeared, more melodies than they could supply. Then nothing deterred them from taking themes of classical music—which they called highbrow —and distorting them into grotesque nightmares of sound; for jazz is a nervous music expressing a nervous age, and it is, too often, the steady effort of the "lowbrow" to out-blare and out-blow.

(However, the term *highbrow* and *lowbrow* might better be dropped, for they both produce a feeling of antagonism. It would be better to use the words they stand for, which are *sincere* and *insincere*, or *educated* and *uneducated*.)

In America, where music developed first as an industry rather than as an art, the popular music was naturally the most flourishing. Only within the last few generations has American wealth, through organizations as well as through individual patrons, been able to encourage composers of serious music. And now, as all things blend in a melting-pot, the jazz characteristics and rhythms are being utilized by many of the living composers of serious music.

The "best" in music, as in all art, lasts as long as there are people to listen and understand. That is why the "best" is always the so-called *serious* music. It is too bad that there is not another and better word for such music, because the word *serious* is misleading. It makes us feel as if we must pull a long face and never smile. That is not the case. Some serious music is as bright and merry as a sunbeam, full of chuckles, and as light as thistle-down. One might call it lasting music, inasmuch as it is the popular music which lasts only until the fashion changes. Whatever is popular in music, clothes, or lines of automobiles, is the fancy of the moment. The popular music which was in fashion when ladies wore bustles and rode about in horse-drawn carriages, was altogether different from the popular music of automobile days and sports clothes.

The minstrel shows were the forerunners of the variety show and vaudeville, and of our present-day musical comedies. Their music was the ancestor of jazz. The jazz spirit, as manifested in painting, sculpture, literature, first appeared in Europe. But America supplied the name to that spirit when it was here developed in music. In Mozart's time, music meant the harmony of consonant sounds. Today, dissonant sounds and even noises are found under the name of music.

[164]

WILLIAM C. HANDY

"No excellence without great labor."

—McGuffey's Fifth Reader

A hundred years have not yet passed away since colored people were owned as slaves by white masters in the United States. Some white people were good to their slaves; others were hard masters. Sometimes a white master would let a slave go free. Christopher Brewer was a Negro who was given his freedom in this way, but as a result of kind treatment preferred, of his own free will, to remain near his former master as a trusted servant. Before he "got religion," he used to play the fiddle for dancing, and his master permitted him to keep the money he earned by his playing. In those days, when Negroes joined a church or, as they called it, "got religion," they felt that dance music and instruments were wrong. After he joined the church, Christopher Brewer laid his fiddle aside, and played no more. His daughter, Elizabeth, loved the music of a guitar, but, being a church member, was never permitted to play it.

A slave named William Wise Handy was not so fortunate as Christopher Brewer. He and his two brothers, longing for freedom, ran away from their masters. There was a chase. The two brothers escaped, but William was caught, sold again as a slave, and taken farther south. In Alabama, he was shot in a second attempt to escape, but he was not killed. He lived to endure the pain of seeing one of his sons, named Hanson, sold away from him "into" Arkansas. Hanson was never heard of again.

Under slavery, the colored families were often separated. Parents lost their children; brothers and sisters were sold away from each other. It is no wonder that the greatest event in history for these people was the surrender of the Southern General, Lee, to the Northern General, Grant, since this marked the beginning of their freedom.

Even as a slave, William Handy worked and studied. He built a log cabin on a site that became known as Handy's Hill, in Florence, Alabama. The kitchen in the cabin had a dirt floor, which he beat down until it looked like asphalt. He attained the respect of the white citizens of the locality, and after the colored people were given their freedom, was the first one to own property in Florence. Then he became a Methodist minister. His son, Charles, also a minister, married Elizabeth Brewer. Though Charles later built a better home for his wife and children, their son, William Christopher, named for both of his grandfathers, was born in the log cabin. He was born, as they said, "eight years after surrender." As he grew up, he was naturally supposed to become a minister, too, but he became what his family considered to be just the opposite—a musician. This was the boy who was to write music called the "blues." It was not easy, however, and there were many heartaches and hardships along the way.

The young boy, whose parents had so recently been freed from slavery, was not himself free to have all the music he wanted. But he loved it from the beginning, and he appreciated keenly all the sounds he heard in nature. They affected his moods, and he would become depressed by the night noises of owls, bats and whip-poorwills. He learned that owls would fly away from the vicinity of a house where a poker had been placed in the fire. So he could drive the owls away by putting a poker in the fire. At the age of six, he entered the Florence District School for Negroes, and soon was taught how to read music.

In church, from the time he was a baby, the boy William heard the spontaneous singing of the spirituals. He came to notice that his father used to cry "whenever anyone raised the familiar spiritual, *March Along, I'll See You on the Judgment Day.*" When he asked his father why he cried, he was told, "That is what the slaves sang when the white folks sold brother Hanson away."

William's teacher in school, though regarding musicians as idlers and wasters, was himself fond of singing. Therefore the time that was devoted every morning in most schools to prayers and scripture reading, was given over in William's school to singing and music instruction. The pupils learned to read their notes by the *do-re-mi* syllables. There was no piano or organ in school, but the teacher used a tuning fork pitched to *A*. To this the pupils sang *la,* and from there they found the note upon which the song began. With their books held in their left hands, beating time with the right, they sang the Gospel hymns as well as their instruction books. They sang through harder books each year, and in time they were singing excerpts from Wagner, Bizet and Verdi. Their part singing was good for ear-training and harmony. To William, this was the best time in school, and he began eagerly to learn how to write music down on paper almost as soon as he knew how to read it.

Being a child of his race, there was no need to study rhythm; he had it by nature. His grandfather Brewer had explained how, in his "sinful" days when he had played the fiddle for dancing, the music-makers used to "bear down" with an intensified rhythm to make the music "hot." At such times, "a boy would stand behind the fiddler with a pair of knitting needles in his hands. From this position the youngster would reach around the fiddler's left shoulder and beat on the strings in the manner of a snare drummer." Some years later, an old man who had remained all his life an expert fiddler and "stomper," showed William just how such music was played. He even allowed William to "handle the needles" while he himself played the violin. The stomping was a particular kind of tapping with the feet with which the Negro dance-fiddlers accompanied their playing and dancing. A good player for dancing, like "Uncle Whit" (as he was called) not only sang while he played but was capable of keeping up an intricate stomping, so that he gave out his music actually from head to foot. Mr. Handy remembers that in those days, "country gals and their suitors got as much enjoyment out of a fiddle at a breakdown or square dance as jitterbugs . . . get nowadays from a swing band."

While he was a young boy, however, William was not allowed to play with "Uncle Whit." That only came later. He had a real uncle who was so strict that he would not permit his own sons even to whistle. When William's grandmother suggested that his large ears indicated a talent for music, he was delighted, but it was the nearest approach to encouragement that he ever received from his family. By the time he was about ten, the sounds of nature and the outdoors became marked in his imagination as notes of music. Even the bellow of a bull impressed itself upon his mind as a musical note, and after he was grown up he recorded this impression when he wrote the *Hooking Cow Blues.*

Though his grandfather Handy died before William was two years old, he never forgot what a white gentleman had later said to him: "Sonny, if you become like your grandfather you will be a great man."

There was plenty of food in the Handy home, but if the boy wanted any money for himself, he had to earn it. It was necessary to have "a nickel for Sunday School and a dime for the church collection." He once traded a gallon of milk for a copy of Benjamin Franklin's *Poor Richard's Almanac*. He collected old iron and rags which he sold. He also sold berries and fruits which he picked in the summer, and nuts gathered in the fall. He learned to make soap from bones which he found in the woods. By pouring rain water over the ashes of hickory wood he could add the necessary lye to the bones. After his soap was boiled down and cold he cut it into cakes and sold it. His father was pleased to see these proofs of his son's industry. He tried to teach the boy to plough, but William had "no luck" with horses or mules.

He was twelve when a friend found him a job as water boy in a rock quarry near Muscle Shoals. William earned fifty cents a day there. He heard the steel drivers sing:

> Oh, baby, 'member las' winter?
> Wasn't it cold—hunh?
> Wasn't it cold—hunh?

In this work-song, the *hunh* was a musical grunt which the workers made when striking with a hammer, or when tugging on a line or lifting a dead weight which required an effort made at the same instant by several men together. Among William Handy's other activities as time went on, he served as an apprentice in shoemaking, carpentry and plastering. At one time, he operated a printing press. And always, there was the inevitable working in the fields—picking cotton, pulling fodder, and cradling oats, millet and wheat. With his earnings he bought his own clothes, books, and school supplies.

As he approached the age of fourteen, William was seized with a great longing. He wanted to play a guitar. But where was he to find the guitar? He would have to save his pennies and buy his own. It was not easy. Though he sometimes made three dollars a week, he divided his earnings into three parts and gave one to his mother, one to his father, and kept the third part for himself. Out of this he had to buy his own necessities, so that it was a year, at least, before he was able to procure the coveted instrument.

When William set his mind on having a musical instrument, it "was like falling in love. All the world seemed bright and changed." In the book in which he has written the story of his life,* Mr. Handy remembers that during the time he wanted the guitar, he paid "more attention to the birds and the riotous carnival they held among the trees." About them, he says "something sang in me and I felt drawn to them." He wanted to play the sounds he heard. He worked harder than ever because it was all working towards the day when he could go and buy the guitar. Even so, the time seemed to drag.

In the store-window he saw and selected the instrument his heart desired. He used to go and stand in

* "Father of the Blues: An Autobiography," by W. C. Handy. 1941. Facts and quotes from this book in the following pages are used by permission of the author and the Macmillan Company.

[171]

front of the window, gazing lovingly upon what would some day surely be his. He could tell no one of his yearning. But his father, noticing the boy's "mooning," sensed that something was wrong, and tried to do little things to please him. He took his son to a creek to teach him how to swim. William didn't learn to swim, however, until later when he was by himself one day, and he jumped into a deep and treacherous water hole. It was then a case of sink or swim. His father also gave him an old Civil War musket which he learned to shoot, though he preferred to hunt with bow and arrow.

When a trumpet player came to town to play with the white Baptist choir, William was seized with the desire for owning a trumpet. He tried to make one by hollowing out a cow horn, and "cutting the tip into a mouthpiece." His result served as a hunting horn but not a trumpet, so he concentrated more than ever on saving pennies for the guitar.

In the springtime, when the doors and windows of the schoolroom were open, William heard from over the fields the song of a Negro ploughman:

> Aye-oh-you, Aye-oh-O,
> I wouldn't live in Cairo-O!

The worksongs of the fields, smelting furnace, and quarry, the spirituals in church, together with the music in school and that which the Handy's Hill youngsters invented, made up the melodies and rhythms which the Negro boy stored away in his memory. These were the musical ingredients that were to reappear, later, when William Handy wrote his Blues.

There came a day in his middle 'teens when William had enough money saved up in small change to go to the department store and buy his guitar. The long-looked-for moment had come at last. He walked on air as he bore his shining new instrument home to show his admiring family. They would be proud of him, he was certain, proud that he had been able to earn it all by himself. When he came into the house and held the guitar up for their inspection, he was so happy that he could not speak. But as no one else spoke first, he finally said,

"Look at it shine. . . . It belongs to me—*me*. I saved up the money."

Then his father spoke. But alas, it was not in terms of praise or pleasure. He was outraged.

"A box," he gasped. "A guitar! One of the devil's playthings. Take it away, I tell you! Get it out of your hands. Whatever possessed you to bring a sinful thing like that into our Christian home? Take it back where it came from. You hear?"

William heard. He was stunned. He wanted to explain that there could be no wrong in having a guitar, but his father had been brought up to think otherwise. Instinctively he felt that it would be utterly impossible to persuade his father to allow him to keep it. He said, weakly, that he didn't think the store would take it back. But his father said:

"They'll exchange it. For the price of a thing like that you could get a new Webster's Unabridged Dictionary—something that'll do you some good."

Sore at heart, the boy exchanged his guitar for the dictionary. His only lessons on an instrument after this episode were those he had on an old organ—lessons in sacred music for which his father paid.

There was something else he liked to do, which was also denied him. He liked to draw. His teacher permitted the drawing of maps, but when William sketched people, which he preferred, he was switched for it.

He began to arrange parts for mixed vocal quartets. At sixteen, he arranged a quartet for women's voices. He was eighteen when another great influence came into his life.

Jim Turner came to Florence. His violin playing was the best that had ever been heard in the town. It made a deep impression on William Handy. Jim brought him a glimpse of another world. Jim organized an orchestra and taught dancing. He knew all the dances of the day. He told stories about Beale Street in Memphis, "where life was a song from dawn to dawn." He described "dark-town dandies and high-brown belles." These stories made William discontented; he wanted to get away, to go places and to see the gay life of Beale Street. He little knew then that some day he would be known by almost all Americans of his race as the author of the *Memphis Blues* and

Beale Street Blues; that he would remember his fiddling friend in the *Joe Turner Blues.*

Towards the end of his school years, a circus stranded in Florence. The white bandmaster tried to earn money by teaching a colored band. The lessons were held in the barber shop. Every afternoon, on his way home from school, William stopped by the barber shop to look through the window and learn the fingering of the various instruments, which the teacher had written on a blackboard. At school he practiced the fingering on his desk. Not long afterwards, when he acquired a cornet, he already knew the fingering.

Playing the cornet, it was natural that he should soon be playing in the band. For his first engagement, playing out of town with Jim Turner's band, he made eight dollars. Receiving so much for what was a day of pleasure to him, as compared with the three dollars which he made for a week's hard labor, made it all the more tempting to give his time to music, though it was against his father's wishes.

After he finished school at eighteen, William's years of wandering began. First he taught music in the town of Bessemer, and then worked in a foundry, as it paid higher wages. In Bessemer, he organized and taught his first brass band. Times grew harder; factories shut down and there was no work. He moved on to Birmingham. Hearing that there was to be a World's Fair in Chicago, he thought it might provide an opportunity for work; and, with the Lauzetta Quartet, he started for Chicago. It was slow going. Singing along the way whenever anyone would engage them, they traveled on freight trains, and slept in box cars or rode "blind baggage." They reached Chicago finally, only to discover that the Fair had been postponed for a year. Thinking to find musical opportunities in St. Louis, they set out again. Once a man gave them a ride which was in itself suspicious. Arriving at the destination the man explained that he was being paid so much a head for every Negro he induced to come to the town to work in a gravel pit. The man did not care whether they stayed or not, since he earned his fee when they stepped off the train.

Upon reaching St. Louis, the quartet was forced to disband. There were many unemployed musicians. The city was affected by hard times. Though William Handy found work for two weeks, he was cheated out of his wages by a contractor of his own race. Then he reached his lowest depths. He knew what it meant to sleep in vacant lots, and on the cobblestones of the Mississippi levee. He was not alone in his wretchedness, there were hundreds of penniless people, both black and white. Sometimes he slept in a chair in a poolroom, but it was a hazardous procedure since the police were constantly watching for vagrants. In order not to be caught and arrested, one's eyes had to be open or a foot must be moving. Handy learned to sleep and keep a foot moving at the same time. He says that two popular songs grew out of the cruelty of the police in those days. Years later, he felt that the misery he endured at that time bore fruit in song. When, sometime afterwards, he sat down at a piano, he produced the *St. Louis Blues* in a single evening. It came easily "out of nowhere."

He need not have borne those hardships, for he could have returned home to Florence. But remembering his father's feeling about music, and that his schoolteacher had once said to him, "What can music do but bring you to the gutter?" he felt that the "I told you so's" which would certainly greet him there, would be far worse than his penniless state. He had passed through towns during his travels North and South, where signs were displayed, saying, "Nigger don't let the sun go down on you here." In times to come, when he sang and played, "I hate to see the evenin' sun go down," it came from an experience deep in his heart.

When William Handy "hoboed" his way to Indiana, his luck changed suddenly. In Evansville he found work easily with a company engaged in repaving a street. He was hungry. When the other men stopped for lunch, a kindly "boss" discovered that the new workman had no money, and loaned him some. Good treatment and agreeable food made him feel better. He found several men working in the same group who were from his home town. They pooled their expenses and managed to live on a dollar a week. Handy looked about and discovered that there were several brass bands in town. He was present at all parades, concerts and rehearsals. Before long he was playing with the Hampton Band, and then his playing was soon observed and people were talking about it.

When Handy was engaged to play for a barbecue in Henderson, Kentucky, his life changed from that of a hobo to a professional musician. He was happy now, after his hard times had come to an end. Kentucky seemed "fresh and green and full of music." He bought a book on harmony and an encyclopedia of music. He also met Elizabeth Price, the girl whom he later married. In Henderson there was a German singing society of several hundred voices. In order to hear the singing and to watch the leader's methods, Handy obtained the work of janitor in the hall. When he received a letter from a musician with whom he had formerly played, giving him an offer to come to Chicago and play cornet with the band of Mahara's Minstrels, he was there in two days. The country was still suffering from a financial depression, so that his wages were only six dollars a week including meals. But as he played more instruments, trained a quartet, and arranged the orchestrations for accompanying the singers, raises in his salary followed. Soon he was able to buy a new trumpet, and he began practicing, as he says, "like an archangel from four to six hours a day."

After the election of President McKinley, prosperity came to the country—and also to William Handy. He bought himself some smart clothes, and naturally he felt better than during the hard times in St. Louis when he had had to button his coat around him because there was no shirt underneath. When he was offered the leadership of one of the Minstrel's two bands, and had a bright uniform to wear, it seemed too good to be true.

Mahara's Minstrel was a Negro minstrel with white management. Their days began just before noon, when the minstrel company paraded in the town which was to see their performance in the evening. The manager blew the whistle in the theatre at a quarter to twelve as a signal for the parade to start. If the company arrived late in town from the place where they had performed the night before, the parade would start directly from the railroad track. The parade was headed by the managers riding in carriages drawn by four horses. They tipped their silk hats with a fine flourish to the citizens standing along the streets. In the second carriage rode the "stars." The "walking-gents" followed, that exciting company which included singers, comedians and acrobats. Then came the drum-major, who sometimes stole the show with his fancy marching, and then—the band. The parade circled the public square, and the band played a program of classical overtures and popular airs. They often played Sousa marches. A piece which was much used because it was always liked, was a selection of tunes entitled *Brudder Gardner's Picnic.* Its tunes were those of Stephen Foster.

After the band played, there were special features —perhaps a trick cyclist—and a speech followed which was to entice the townspeople to the evening perfor-

[179]

mance. After this, the members of the troupe were free until seven-thirty in the evening when the band played again in front of the local opera-house.

For many years, Handy traveled with minstrel shows. His travels took him all over the country, from Cuba to California; from Canada to Mexico. During these years, he was married, and his wife went with him. In Cuba, he was fascinated by the rhythms of the strange native airs, especially those he heard from "shy bands" which played behind closed shutters in back streets. Thirty years later, these were the rhythms which were heard in New York and throughout the country as the Rumba.

A number in the show was a cornet solo played by Handy. Once when Mahara's Minstrels played in Alabama, William Handy's father came to see his son perform. It was a great moment for William, who knew what the effort had cost his father in thus overcoming his prejudice. Father Handy was pleased at William's success, and proudly boasted to other listeners that the leader of the band was his son. After the curtain fell, the father went up to the son and shook hands, saying, "Sonny, I haven't seen a show since I professed religion. I enjoyed it. I am very proud of you and forgive you for becoming a musician."

The Handys were back in Florence when their first child was born, and William and Jim Turner organized a small orchestra. As a result of playing a concert at which the president of the Agricultural and Mechanical

College was present, William Handy was invited, at the age of twenty-seven, to become the director of the band, orchestra, and vocal music at the College. Accepting that position, he then had a home of his own for the first time.

Ragtime music was coming in fashion. For a long while, American music, as well as the ragtime of Negro origin, was looked down upon in this country. Foreign music was preferred even though it might be inferior. Handy resented the insincerity of such judgment. For a concert, he rewrote *My Ragtime Baby* and gave it a classical-sounding name for his band to play. It received much applause; even the College President complimented Handy on the piece. From the first, Handy promoted ragtime as much as he could. Receiving a small salary at the College, Handy decided after two years that he was worth more, and inserted an advertisement in a popular Negro newspaper. Thereupon he found himself again with Mahara's Minstrels, though by that time it was the beginning of the end for the minstrel show.

Mr. Handy says, "Southern Negroes sing about everything." They can make songs about trains, steamboats, sledge hammers, mean bosses and stubborn mules. They can accompany their songs on anything from which they can get a musical sound or a rhythmic effect, "from a harmonica to a washboard"; and of such materials came the blues.

There was a time when Handy, studying his har-

[181]

mony book and music encyclopedia which he had bought in Henderson, thought that everything most important came from books. Even he had regarded the primitive music of his own people with scorn. He felt that the simple form of endless repetition was much too simple. But he came to realize that although the music of the blues did not come from books, the ordinary everyday experiences simply expressed by lowly people in primitive song gave a sincerity that was appealing.

One evening while playing for a dance in a town in Mississippi he learned his greatest lesson. A request was made for some of "our native music." His musicians at that time were not minstrel men who could, as he says, "fake and sell" their music; they had to play according to printed notes. They played an old-time Southern tune, a melody more sophisticated than native. But another request came, asking if they would object if a local colored band played a few dances. On the contrary, they were glad to hear the others play. Whereupon three country lads with ill-fitting clothes shambled out with their instruments—"a battered guitar, a mandolin and a worn-out bass. The music they made was pretty well in keeping with their looks. They struck up one of those over-and-over strains that seem to have no very clear beginning and certainly no end at all. The strumming attained a disturbing monotony, but on and on it went, a kind of stuff that has long been associated with cane rows and levee camps. Thump-thump-thump went their feet on the floor. Their eyes rolled. Their shoulders swayed. And through it all that little agonizing strain persisted. It was not really annoying or unpleasant. Perhaps *haunting* is a better word."

As William Handy listened to the endless little tune, he wondered if anybody besides the country bumpkins could possibly care for it. He learned better when he saw the rain of silver dollars which began to fall around the stomping feet. The dancers went wild. Those country black boys taught Handy something which he could not, he feels, have learned from books. It was then that he saw the beauty of primitive music, and "that night a composer was born." He went home to work on that kind of music. He had long felt that the American people wanted rhythm and movement in their dance music.

When Handy orchestrated some of the local tunes, and played for dances in the magnificent plantation mansions of the delta country of Mississippi, and for political rallies, he made more money than he had ever earned before.

He was in Memphis again in 1909, when he wrote a piece about Mr. Crump for his band to play during a political campaign. He was in his thirties then. Under a different title, *Memphis Blues*, it was published three years later—the first of the many published blues which followed, and therefore a pioneering work. He began to write many songs, and the blues came more and more frequently.

It was also in Memphis where Handy met Harry H. Pace, cashier of a Negro bank, who had musical leanings. He had written some song lyrics, and was much in demand as a singer on church programs. The two men collaborated on songs, and became partners in a music-publishing house, called the Pace and Handy Music Company.

When Mr. Handy was forty-five, his publishing firm moved from Beale Street to Broadway. Ragtime music was now called jazz. Songs were rolling out of Tin Pan Alley. After years of ups and downs—downs which included for the blues writer a period of blindness—money began to pour in from the recording companies. William Handy was invited to conduct his blues on programs in New York. At the end of the Great War, when jazz was "coming in," Handy's blues were played by an American Negro band in Paris. American white soldiers were thrilled, recognizing it as music from home. Though, as Mr. Handy says, "the blues were all born humble" they came to be played, finally, in concert halls. Paul Whiteman played and made a record of his orchestral arrangement of Handy's *St. Louis Blues*. At a Hippodrome concert in New York, when Whiteman's band played, Deems Taylor delivered the Living Program Notes. The blues of Handy were played for King Edward VIII of England. An authority on the subject feels that the *Memphis* and *St. Louis Blues* contributed more to the début of jazz than any other individual composition. The *St. Louis Blues*, written in 1914, was so successful that it was still netting $25,000 a year forty-two years later!

After reaching the age of seventy and with failing eyesight, Mr. Handy still went every day to his office on Broadway. He could still entertain soldiers and sailors during World War II. Up in his seventies, and blind, the man who had once been a water-boy, a shoemaker, a cotton-picker, a steel-worker, and successful blues writer, was still playing his golden trumpet, upon occasion, in Billy Rose's Diamond Horseshoe. A dinner was given in his honor at the Waldorf to celebrate his seventy-eighth birthday. At eighty, the "Father of the Blues" played for hundreds of Brooklyn high school children. After their wild applause, he patted his trumpet and said, "Life is something like this trumpet. If you don't put anything in it, you don't get anything out."

Mr. Handy felt that Nevin's song *Mighty Lak' a Rose* did much in creating a favorable sentiment for his race. Through the years he remembered the lessons from *McGuffey's Fifth Reader*, for he learned in the hard school of experience the truth quoted at the head of this chapter.

William Christopher Handy, born on Handy's Hill,
Florence, Alabama, November 16, 1873.
Died in New York, March 28, 1958.

CHARLES EDWARD IVES

"Pa taught me what I know."

"Pa" was a bandmaster in Danbury, Connecticut, where Charles Ives was born in 1874. Other people knew "Pa" as George Ives, a musician who was the leader of all musical activities in the town. Besides being a bandmaster, choir leader, and teacher who taught many of the young people to know good music, he was vastly interested and curious about the science of sound, studied acoustics and even invented an instrument that would give him quarter tones.

As a lad of sixteen George Ives had organized a Civil War Army Band. When the First Connecticut Heavy Artillery Band, led by him, passed in review during the siege of Richmond, President Lincoln was heard to observe, "That's a good band." General Grant replied that he had heard that it was the best band in the army, though he himself was incapable of judging because the only tune he could recognize was *Yankee Doodle.*

Later, in New York, George Ives had known Stephen Foster. When his boy Charles was five, he began to give him music lessons. He started all his children —and many of the children in the town—on Bach and Stephen Foster. Not only was he open-minded about trying out new musical possibilities, but he taught his boy not to be afraid of doing unconventional things with music. When Charles was only ten, his father had him sing *Swanee River* in the key of E-flat while playing the accompaniment in C. The purpose, he said, was to "stretch our ears." For a man with absolute pitch, this was indeed stretching, and it shows that Charles must also have possessed a keen sense of pitch.

If Mr. George Ives could have lived about fifty years longer, he might have felt well rewarded to find his son Charles hailed as the most original of American composers, while his compositions were held in highest esteem by musicians and critics, both at home and abroad.

One day when Charles was eight years old, his father, seeing that the child was fascinated by the drummer's rhythms in the band, took him to the village barber, who had played the drums in Ives's Civil War Band. The barber sat Charlie down before an empty tub, gave him a pair of drumsticks, and proceeded to teach him, between the shaves and hair-cuts, how to manipulate the double-roll. At twelve, Charles could play the snare drum in the band.

By the time he was thirteen, he was accomplished enough in music to become the organist of the West Street Congregational Church of Danbury. That year, he also wrote a band piece, called *Holiday Quick Step*, but he was too shy to play with the others when his proud father first had it played in the Decoration Day parade. When the band come marching down the street, past his house, young Ives was out back by himself, throwing a

[187]

baseball against the barn door and catching it. But a local critic predicted a brilliant future for the young organist and composer.

Charles went to the Danbury Public Schools and then to the Hopkins Grammar School, to prepare for Yale. At Yale, he took academic and music courses, studying organ with Dudley Buck and composition with Horatio Parker. He also played the organ in New Haven churches until he graduated in 1898. He still had time to play baseball and football.

Before he received his degree, however, Charles Ives was already writing a composition for organ which contained deliberate discords, or what were then considered impossible chord combinations. A few years later, Stravinsky and Schönberg were to cause great excitement in the musical world by such consciously daring writing. But, quietly and by himself, Ives was already experimenting in ear-stretching sounds, though he had never then so much as heard of Stravinsky and Schönberg. Ives is now credited with being the first to use polyharmony (more than one key at the same time) and atonality (with the keys wild, as it were, with no home base).

Horatio Parker, an excellent musician and a proper composer of the European nineteenth-century school, was not in sympathy with his pupil's new-fangled sounds; and, after he asked Charles if he must "hog all the keys," Charles knew better than to show his teacher all of his compositions. To most people who heard his music for the first time, it sounded "outlandish." It was not the kind of music in which people had come to feel at home. He used unusual chord structures, queer scale passages, wide melodic skips, interwoven textures of rhythms, all of which vexed his teachers, who taught the conventional European music. Some of these musical ideas were not really so new as they seemed. They had been used in tribal music and in the distant past, but they were new to modern American and European ears, and to the young composer himself. There are always some people, however, whose minds are awake to new things. Musicians who were looking forward to experiments found young Ives' music worth noticing.

After he finished college, the young part-time composer held positions as organist and choir director in churches in New Jersey and New York City for some years, but his daily work was not in music. Upon graduating, he decided to enter the insurance business and became a clerk for the Mutual Life Insurance Company. Insurance work appealed to him, and he wanted most of all to be free to write the kind of music he liked. After some years, he established the firm of Ives and Company, and a few years after that, he and another clerk became managers for Mutual. Their firm, Ives and Myrick, had grown to be one of the largest of its kind in the country when it was dissolved, twenty-one years later, because Charles Ives was forced to retire on account of poor health.

He was highly esteemed in his business, and showed

as much initiative there as he did in music. He was a pioneer in some new insurance ideas, and during twenty-one years, his firm placed new business in Mutual to the amount of $450,000,000. He said, "My business experience revealed life to me in many aspects that I might otherwise have missed. In it one sees tragedy, nobility, meanness, high aims, low aims, brave hopes, faint hopes, great ideals, no ideals, and one is able to watch these work inevitable destiny."

Ten years after his college days were over, Ives married a girl whose first name was Harmony. She lived up to her name for him. She did not mind that, during all the years when her husband worked in an office by day, he spent his evenings, weekends, and vacations at home writing music. And she never asked him to write something "nice" that people would like; she understood that he must write what was within him. He said later that they never went anywhere and she didn't mind. And he told a friend that his debt to his wife was as great as his debt to his father. She was the daughter of an eminent Hartford clergyman who had known Mark Twain, Whittier, Harriet Beecher Stowe, and all of the literary persons of the community. He had, in fact, been Mark Twain's traveling companion in "A Tramp Abroad."

As the years went by, Ives piled up many compositions. In 1920, he had his volume of 114 songs privately printed and distributed. The next year, his *Concord Sonata* for piano was printed. Musicians were at once greatly impressed, especially the younger ones, who were more interested in the new music. But though musicians and critics alike praised his compositions, many more years went by before Ives's name became well-known. He did not attempt to push his music at the public; his music was very difficult to play; it was not the kind to make an instant appeal. It was not pretty or easy to understand—it was what he called "strong" music.

After the scholarly pianist, John Kirkpatrick, had studied Ives's *Concord Sonata* for twelve years (at the beginning even he could not understand it), he played it in New York in 1929. The response was highly gratifying, and he repeated the *Thoreau* movement as an encore. Critics were in accord as to the importance of this music. One called it the greatest yet composed by an American. A few weeks later, the pianist repeated it by public demand, presenting an all-Ives program to a sold-out house. Thirty-five years after Ives had finished his Third Symphony, it was performed for the first time in 1946, winning the Pulitzer Prize.

Most composers feel that what they have written must not be changed in any way in performance. But we live in a time of "arrangements" and Mr. Ives felt, when he published his 114 Songs over thirty years ago, that as far as his music was concerned, anyone who wanted it should be free to use it, copy it, transpose it or arrange it for other instruments. He even objected to his publishers' copyrighting his music, believing that anyone should have free access to it. Finally he agreed to the usual procedure, but on condition that any profits his music earned be used in publishing music of young composers. He may have "hogged" the keys, as his teacher put it, but he did not make any reservations about his music or his rights.

After many years of devoted and loving work in all his free time from the insurance business, the number of compositions by Ives mounted to a large figure. He has written several symphonies, chamber works, choral works, songs, and piano compositions. Some of his passages have been called indescribably beautiful, and his work as a whole has been called the most significant, most truly national, yet written by an American. In his music, the composer's intense love for his country, idealism, admiration for the high points of his country's past are manifested, as well as his dear memories of his boyhood's musical experiences. Besides the music his father taught him, these memories held the music a Connecticut Yankee of the 1870's and 1880's would have heard: the music of the old barn dances; revival meetings; Memorial Day Parades; minstrel airs; harvesttime singing; the old village fiddler, with his slips and slides and off-pitch tunes; the town band with its hearty blare, in which—if the players were feeling independent or inspired, or sometimes, perhaps, careless—the accents would be in the wrong places and the band itself not quite together in time or in tone; the wheezy little church organ or harmonium, perhaps out of tune, its notes swelling and dimming in unexpected places, when the bellows lacked air or filled too suddenly; the singing of the congregation, with some voices dragging, some hurrying, some sharp, some flat, but singing with an ardent self-assurance. All these, and the ear-stretching exercises went into the music of Charles Ives, America's most original and important national composer.

Charles Edward Ives, born in Danbury, Connecticut, October 20, 1874. Died in New York, May 19, 1954.

CHARLES TOMLINSON GRIFFES

"A fastidious craftsman, a scrupulous artist."

—LAWRENCE GILMAN

Wilbur Griffes was a business man who lived in Elmira, New York. He and his wife had literary tastes and they were also very fond of music. They had five children who learned to play musical instruments; and the third child, a boy named Charles, became a composer.

A child prodigy is about as rare as a genius. None of the composers whose stories are written here were child prodigies. But without being a genius, a man can produce work so valuable that it lives on after he is gone. Charles Griffes was not a prodigy, but even as a child he had a feeling that he was meant to do something out of the ordinary.

One of his sisters was a violinist; another, older than he, was not only a pianist but also a teacher of piano, and it was from her that he had his first lessons while still quite young. Showing an aptitude for music, he did not have to work at it in spite of parents' wishes to the contrary, as several other composers had to do when they were young. It was natural that, in such a home, Charles should have been encouraged in his artistic tendencies, and that he should have early acquired a fondness for reading.

Books of travel appealed to him, especially. He loved to think about far-off places. He was fascinated by the countries of the Orient. He also enjoyed reading poetry and for a time the American poet, Edgar Allan Poe, was his favorite. Later, when Charles grew up, these tendencies were to blossom in his musical compositions.

In drawing and in the painting of water-colors he became very adept—an ability we have noted in several other composers. As Charles Griffes grew older, he made some fine etchings on copper, and he was even urged by some people to make painting his life-work.

He went to the public school and liked it. He played games, and was especially fond of tennis. Charles was not the hearty type of boy who accepted everyone, willy-nilly, as a friend; he was reserved. He cherished his own few close friends. He began, as a young boy, to compose songs and pieces for the piano, which were performed in Elmira.

Charles' second teacher in piano was an accom-plished pianist, Mary S. Broughton, who had been trained in Germany. He was given the best music of the greatest masters to study, and thus his musical taste was developed. At a time when he was much interested in reading romantic poetry and prose, his own compositions reflected a light, romantic style. Later he was much impressed by the music of Richard Strauss, Hugo

Wolf and Brahms. During his years in high school, Charles' piano-playing became better and better, and his teacher advised him to go to Berlin to continue his education in music.

At nineteen, therefore, Charles set off for Germany with the idea of becoming a concert pianist. He also studied musical theory and composition. One of his teachers in composition was Humperdinck, the composer of *Hänsel and Gretel.* Though Griffes was in Germany when the craze for Wagner's music was flourishing, he was able to keep a clear head. He liked the music of Wagner well enough, but he was not swept away by it. When he was twenty, he played for the first time in public in Berlin, performing a sonata for piano which he had written.

While he was in Germany, Griffes' ambition changed its goal. Instead of being a concert pianist, he would become a composer. Though he studied and read other foreign languages, he came, naturally, to know German best. He set five German poems to music, and these songs were his first compositions to be published. They were published when he was twenty-five after he returned to his own country. He studied four years in Germany, and also did some teaching there.

When he came home, it was necessary to find work, since it was not possible for a serious composer to earn a living by his own writing. He became choir-master and teacher of piano at the Hackley School for Boys in Tarrytown. In his spare time he studied the music which was being written, especially the modern (as it was called then) French and Russian music, and continued to write his own. He would have liked to put all his time on study and composition; and therefore teaching became irksome, and he did not enjoy it.

During the thirteen years he taught at Tarrytown, he wrote the compositions for which he is now remembered. Of the set of four pieces for piano called *Roman Sketches*, the most played is *The White Peacock*. Griffes himself was very fond of the music he wrote for a ballet, *The Kairn of Koridwen*, which was performed by the Neighborhood Playhouse in New York. His ballet, *Sho-jo*, written about a legendary dance of old Japan, achieved enough popularity to be performed in New York, Boston, and on tour. Being still drawn to thoughts of the Orient, he set to music five poems of ancient China and Japan. These songs were written on five-tone and six-tone scales.

Charles Griffes liked to experiment, not only in scales but also in forms. When he wrote his big *Sonata* for piano, he based it on an original scale of his own. The *Sonata* is very difficult, and he was a good pianist himself in order to be able to play it. It was played first at the MacDowell Club in New York by its composer.

The tone poem for orchestra, *The Pleasure Dome of Kubla Khan*, was accepted for performance by the Boston Symphony Orchestra. It received high praise, and at last Griffes not only achieved a triumphant recognition, but was commissioned for further compositions. In the lives of almost all the composers, it is very noticeable how much more eagerly they can write when once they feel that their music is wanted. Encouragement is a spur to greater effort than is possible when a musician is wondering, while he works, if anybody will ever care to listen to his music. When Griffes' *Poem* for flute and orchestra was played by the flutist for whom he had written it, Georges Barrère, it received a tremendous ovation.

Charles Griffes had a delightful sense of humor, and enjoyed friends who were distinguished by their musical or artistic attainments. But his later years were not happy. There was too much uncongenial work in his life; too much time had to be spent on teaching. Then, too, he was not well, and had to be seeing doctors.

He was only in his middle thirties when he died— just when success was definitely coming to him. Deems Taylor wrote about Griffes that, "his early death is . . . the greatest musical loss that this country has sustained." Mr. Taylor thought that Griffes would have become world-famous, and that "his music would be a sign that America had produced a composer of the first rank."

Though Griffes wrote less than forty compositions in all, those mentioned, together with a work for chorus and orchestra, *These Things Shall Be,* and also three pieces for violin and orchestra, *The Lament of Ian the Proud, Thy Dark Eyes to Mine,* and *The Rose of the Night* are his most significant works on which his reputation rests. He wrote a *String Quartet* in which he used an Indian theme, but he did not feel that the Indian theme rendered the work "American" on that account. His works are played in Europe, and sometimes one will meet a European unfamiliar with the names of American composers, who will nevertheless know the name of Charles Griffes.

Charles Tomlinson Griffes, born in Elmira,
New York, September 17, 1884. Died
in New York, April 8, 1920.

JEROME KERN

"I've got something for you."

The year before Victor Herbert came to New York, where he later made his name as a writer of operetta, a boy was born in the same city, who was to share honors in the same musical field with the older composer. Mr. Henry Kern, like Stephen Foster's father, was a merchant. His wife played piano, and when the three Kern boys were old enough to start music, their mother gave them lessons on the piano. There were just enough piano-playing Kerns to play eight-hand arrangements in concerts.

When Jerome Kern was ten, the family moved to Newark. He attended the high school there, played organ in assembly, directed a musical show in school, and graduated at the age of seventeen. He continued to study piano with other teachers and also at the New York College of Music. Then he began to study harmony.

Since music was the thing he wanted most, he asked his father if he might go abroad for further study when he had graduated from high school. Mr. Kern consented. Jerome might go if he wanted to, but his father thought that before making such a step he had better try working in the business for a little while at least. There was just the chance that business might, after all, be the thing for him. So Jerome spent the summer after his graduation, in the Kern merchandizing establishment.

This establishment did not deal in musical instruments, but when Mr. Kern received two orders for pianos he naturally wished to supply them. He assigned his son Jerome to visit a piano factory and buy two pianos. The young boy just out of school went over to New York to "do business." His experience was delightful. The owners of the piano factory were most agreeable gentlemen who, very hospitably, invited him out to lunch. Their manners and conversation were so persuasive that Jerome discovered, when he arose from the lunch-table, that he had bought two hundred pianos!

When he returned to tell his father the result of the day's work, poor Mr. Kern must have heartily wished that his son was abroad studying music. Here he was with two hundred pianos on his hands, and what was he going to do with them? After several days of worry and fuss trying to adjust himself to the new "business," the elder Kern rented a warehouse in which to store his hundred and ninety-eight surplus pianos. By offering them for sale on instalment rates lower than the usual ones, he succeeded before long in disposing of all of them. Not long afterwards, pianos became a main item in the business, but by that time Jerome did not work there anymore. His father was happy to send him abroad to study music.

Later that same year, when he was seventeen, Jerome went to Germany, and the year after that, he had his first musical job. For some time, he alternated jobs in New York and London, with trips to Germany for study. He was a plugger in a music-publishing house about the time when ragtime ushered in a new industry and a new profession. The new slogan was, "Try This on Your Piano."

Less than two hundreds years had passed since the singing-schools which sprang up in New England first gave rise to the "new" profession of singing-teacher who taught people how to read their notes. Then followed a period when visiting artists from Europe, attracted by the gold of a growing country, gave in return for the gold a standard of musical taste. An emphasis on entertainment music followed the settling and growth of the new land. The first entertainment music was as crude as the first serious music had been. The country's wealth and industry brought musical instruments to the fore. Jerome Kern came along just at the time when proficiency in instrumental music was spreading throughout the country, and his great contribution was the refinement of entertainment music.

Kern's career as a composer began when he was eighteen, working as a staff musician for a producer who specialized in importing musical "diversions" from England. In those days it was considered quite the thing in London to arrive late at the musical shows. Mr. Kern now says he owes his start to that peculiar custom! The entertainments were constructed to conform with the fashion. The music "tinkled along monotonously" during the first part of the performance. Not until rather well along in the evening was there a musical number of any importance—not until there was a chance that the audience had arrived and was ready to listen. But in America customs differed. When musical comedies of this sort were given in New York, new openings had to be written for the American audiences who came on time and wanted something worth listening to from the moment the lights went down and the conductor lifted his baton. Jerome Kern was eighteen when he wrote one of these new beginnings for a show imported from London.

The next year he did the same. Frequently his work took him to London. As he continued in this kind of musical patchwork, other people began to notice that the best music in the shows came in the first part— the part which was always composed by Jerome Kern.

When he was twenty-five, he composed an entire score. In the autumn of that same year, he was married, while in England, to an English girl.

The year after, his first original musical comedy was produced. It was called *The Red Petticoat*. He was now a recognized composer, not only on Broadway but in Piccadilly. Soon he was supplying the music for at least one show a year, sometimes for two or three; and shows with "Music by Jerome Kern" were frequently playing at the same time in New York, London,

[203]

and Paris. There was no end to the tunes which came to him; he could just keep on writing them down—only, he had to be careful that he did not copy from himself.

The following ten years, which included the period of the World War, when the twentieth century was in its 'teens, were the years when operetta reached its height. Musical shows were romantic and exotic. Frequently the "stories" were historical. The music was tuneful, the rhythm lilting. Four composers predominated in supplying the demand for this kind of music. They were the Irish-American, Victor Herbert, who wrote *Babes in Toyland;* the Bavarian Rudolph Friml, who wrote *Katinka;* the Hungarian, Sigmund Romberg, who wrote *In Blossom Time;* and the New Yorker, Jerome David Kern, who wrote—to name but a few—*Very Good Eddie, Have a Heart, Leave It to Jane, The Bunch and Judy, Stepping Stones.*

As in the old days when the minstrel shows had grown from the small affairs of Dan Emmett, when his "Big Four" entertainers were enough to delight an audience, to the great shows consisting of forty, or "Sixty, Count 'Em Sixty,"—so the musical comedy shows grew in size until they almost died of their own weight—or expense. Producers vied with each other during the '20's to mount the most costly displays of extravagant magnificence. Fifty thousand dollars did not go far when lavished upon shows that had run to quantity instead of quality; when a hundred chorus girls were more desirable in the eyes of the box-office than fifty;

when eight comedians were considered four times as funny as two; when a dance team was reinforced by a whole dance group. Things were changing in the scene of popular music.

The stories or plots of musical comedy had become things of shreds and patches, and very few of those. The romantic story had disappeared along with the "hero" tradition. There was no more characterization. Music was not written to a musical show; but the story —what there was of it—as well as the music, was "assembled" around the all-important hit-songs which were "spotted" throughout the duration of the "traffic on the stage." People didn't mind. They did not seem to care if they had no well-defined story. A little o' this, and a little o' that sufficed. As for instruments, the graceful strings had been superseded by the wind and percussion instruments because jazz had come in, bringing its uneasy rhythms. What melodies there were, were snappy and broken, written primarily not for the voice but for the feet. The ingratiating melody, no longer wanted, had been forgotten. But, not by Jerome Kern.

In the midst of all the change towards *fortissimo* blare, the song-writer, who never deliberately sat down with the idea of writing a "hit-song," but rather with the idea of writing music to please himself, composed a long flowing line of melody in *Ol' Man River*, which turned out to be the most popular song of the season— indeed of several seasons.

When Miss Edna Ferber's novel, *Show Boat,* was

published, Jerome Kern saw its advertisement in the paper, bought a copy and then couldn't read it. Naturally the author was considerably upset when the composer told her this, but he explained it. As he turned the pages, he said, tune after tune came into his mind so that he had to stop reading and go to the piano continually. He told Miss Ferber that it would make an ideal light opera.

The contract was signed. Oscar Hammerstein wrote the lyrics—after which, Mr. Kern said, "the music wrote itself." Being himself ignorant of life in the South, he turned to a favorite book, Mark Twain's *Life on the Mississippi,* and from it he caught the "rhythmic, wistful melancholy of the Mississippi River Negro." This was what he wrote into *Ol' Man River,* which became the popular hit-song of *Show Boat.* Some critics have said that this is an opera comique in the true classical sense of the term, and the first one which is truly all-American.

Mr. Kern decided to produce his musical plays without chorus girls. He came to consider them out of date. It disturbed him to have them come prancing out on the stage when they had nothing to do with the story, and when, as he said, "they did not even sing well." *The Cat and the Fiddle,* and *Music in the Air* were great successes, though neither of them contained a single chorus girl. *The Cat and the Fiddle* played in cities where a musical play had not been heard for years.

Jerome Kern's gift for characterization and humor,

as well as his ability to write real melody, gave to his music what one writer called a "quality of grace." Having learned musical structure in his early training in Germany, he was able to make his own deviations through the changing fashion in popular music and retain a style of his own. It has been said that Kern liked to write in the manner of Mozart, and that he could compose a fugue. Not many writers of popular music have had such models before them. He has been called "erudite" in the field of popular music. When he wrote musical comedy in England with P. G. Wodehouse, the results were suggestive of the masterpieces of Gilbert and Sullivan.

Mr. Kern was not by any means through with a show when he had written the music. Capable of hard work, he saw his play through the rehearsals himself and attended to every detail in person. When a new melody came to him, he summoned anyone he could find, stagehands or electricians, and going to the piano, he would smile at them, saying:

"I've got something for you."

In the days when the composer lived outside of New York turning out such popular melodies as *They Didn't Believe Me*, and *You're Here and I'm Here*, he used to say that he had none of the eccentricities of an artist or musician—that he was just a hard-working suburbanite who lived simply and was devoted to his wife and daughter. He said, "I have never bought a lot of funny clothes." But just the same, while he was working on *Music in the Air* he bought some Bavarian clothes and appeared in them at the rehearsals.

With the perfecting of sound reproduction in the 'thirties, musicians writing light music were drawn into Hollywood's unparalleled industry. Mr. Kern then lived in California and continued to "give us something" by composing light operas and musical comedies for the screen. He supplied musical rôles for various stars including Lily Pons, Irene Dunne, and Grace Moore.

M. Kern never cared for games—never liked tennis, golf or cards—but he developed one great hobby. He liked to attend book auctions and collect rare books. Sometimes he paid fifteen and twenty thousand dollars for a single rare volume. What's more, he read them. He had acquired a great collection when, the year before prosperity collapsed in 1929, he placed the entire lot on sale. The auction lasted for several days. Many dealers, who had no doubt thought Mr. Kern was an easy mark when he used to enter their shops to buy, attended the sale. Perhaps they had the same opinion about his discretion in buying, as the piano-factory owners and his father had had when he was just out of school. But when the sale was over, it brought the composer a million dollars profit. Moreover, he had had the pleasure of owning the books for a time. He had shown judgment, it appeared, as rare as his books.

Jerome David Kern, born in New York City, January 27, 1885.
Died in New York City, November 11, 1945.

GEORGE GERSHWIN

"I frequently hear music in the very heart of noise."

About the time when American inventions were beginning to speed up American life, and people were anticipating the possibility of speaking to their distant friends through the small mouthpiece of a new device called a telephone, a young girl named Rose Bruskin came from St. Petersburg, Russia, to live in New York. Not long afterwards, a young Jew named Gershwin, of the same Russian city, also arrived in New York—where the streets were soon to be lighted with electricity instead of gas. These two were married when Rose was only sixteen.

In time this pair had four children. When the eldest boy, Isadore, who later became known as Ira, was about two years old there was a baby brother named Jacob. Ira was an East Side boy, but Jacob, who came to use the name of George, was born in Brooklyn, just across the river. Father Gershwin tried his hand at many different kinds of jobs in those years, and the family moved dozens of times. They were back again on the New York side when George was still only a few months old. But wherever they lived, the sidewalks of New York were the playgrounds for these brothers.

George became the roller-skate champion of one

neighborhood where they lived. He was athletic and liked games, a merry fellow who was always on the go. A "city kid," he never knew what it meant to avoid others. He never wanted to go off by himself, there was always a gang to play with. He went to the public schools, but study was a nuisance. He didn't care for reading, except that for a while he liked fairy-tales. He left the reading to Ira, who was fond of thrillers. Music did not mean anything, either—that is, until something happened. In fact, his father thought that George would probably grow up to be a vagabond.

In Public School 20, they sang some of the good old-time songs, such as *Annie Laurie* and *Loch Lomond*. George liked *Loch Lomond*, and Sir Arthur Sullivan's *The Lost Chord*, but he didn't know a thing about music. What he heard was the street hurdy-gurdies grinding out their blatant tunes through the roar of elevated trains overhead, a street singer or fiddler struggling to be heard above the din of traffic, the machine music of the merry-go-rounds of Coney Island and the ragtime of the honkey-tonks. If a boy took lessons on the piano or the violin, George regarded him as just a "little Maggie." No use in being a sissy, thought George. This was because he was absolutely ignorant of what there might be in music, and he knew no musicians or anybody else who might have opened his mind. It is a great thing to remember that such faults as these lie within ourselves. However, we do not usually get awake to these things until we are older. Those who realize early that more interests add more enjoyment to life are usually those who have more opportunities. George Gershwin was rather a bad boy, too, at the start, but he learned.

In those days, many people who didn't know anything about music would buy a piano because someone they knew had bought one. You probably know, even now, some boys or girls who take music lessons because their friend Jack or Nancy takes them, and they don't want to be left out of it. It is strange how most people want to be like everybody else. Few are really independent enough to want to be different. The Gershwins bought a piano because one of their relatives had brought one. It was decided that Ira ought to take lessons.

Ira began, but he didn't last long at it. He preferred to read. He found a circulating library on Broome Street back of a laundry, where the renting of novels of adventure came within his weekly allowance of twenty-five cents. He pored over stories about the *Liberty Boys of '76, Pluck and Luck,* and tales of the Wild West. Sometimes he read as many as ten of these cheap thrillers in a week. He read many he wasn't supposed to read. If he heard one of his parents coming when he was in the midst of a forbidden book, he learned how to hide it in a jiffy under the carpet or behind one of the family pictures on the wall. This was much more exciting to him than tickling the ivory keys of the new piano. He soon found, however, that he was not going to be forced to sit at the piano, because someone else was already there. He was crowded out. And the one who sat on the piano-stool was brother George.

That piano fascinated George. The very boy who didn't want to be a "little Maggie" asked, when he was thirteen, if he might have a piano teacher! Then he seemed to make up for lost time, and worked so assiduously that he wore out his instruction books. Something that happened at school had changed George all around.

A Rumanian boy who also attended the same school played violin at one of the entertainments. George didn't care enough about it to go to assembly hall. He stayed away. Maxie Rosenzweig, who is now the violinist Max Rosen, was a year younger than George and already a very fine player. Down the stairway and through the halls came the strains of Dvořák's *Humoresque,* and in spite of himself, George was drawn to the sweet music as a duck to water.

"It was," he said, later, "a flashing revelation of beauty. I made up my mind to get acquainted with this fellow, and I waited outside from three to four-thirty that afternoon, in the hopes of greeting him. It was pouring cats and dogs, and I got soaked to the skin."

The young violinist did not appear and George went back into the school to find that he had already left. He found out where Max's home was, and, dripping wet, went after him. Again no luck, Max was not at home, either. Max's parents, amused by the eager, dripping George, arranged a meeting and before long the boys were the best of friends. They went about together arm in arm, and wrote letters to each other over Saturdays and Sundays.

"Max opened the world of music to me," said George. "When we'd play hooky together, we'd talk eternally about music—that is, when we weren't wrestling."

The new friend, however, didn't think that George was meant for a musical career, and he said to him, "You haven't it in you, Georgie; take my word for it, I can tell."

But now that music had begun to mean something to George Gershwin, it meant everything. He went after it with might and main. He had several teachers for short periods, one after the other, until he found the right one—the one who was to be the second great musical influence in his life.

The same teacher may not be the right teacher for everybody. Pupils are not all alike. There are differences of personal traits and qualities, and differences in the requirements of a pupil not only in what he needs to be taught but how he needs to be treated. It is the same with friends. Tom will like Dick as well as he likes Harry, and yet Dick and Harry will not be friends at all.

When George Gershwin found Charles Hambitzer, he found his ideal teacher; and Hambitzer felt the same way about his new pupil. He considered him a genius. He said:

"Gershwin is just crazy about music and can't wait

until it's time to take his lesson. No watching the clock for this boy! He wants to go in for this modern stuff, jazz. . . . But I'm not going to let him for a while. I'll see that he gets a firm foundation in the standard music first."

And George said afterwards, "I was crazy about that man. I went out . . . and drummed up ten pupils for him. . . . Under Hambitzer I first became familiar with Chopin, Liszt and Debussy. He made me harmony-conscious."

But he did it by the music he put in George's way, because Mr. Hambitzer never taught him harmony. He was making a pianist of Gershwin. He was pianist, himself, in an orchestra. His great-grandfather had been court violinist to the Czar of Russia. When Hambitzer died as a young man, George felt that he could never again have a teacher who could mean so much to him. And he didn't. He had lessons, later, with other pianists, and also studied harmony under Rubin Goldmark. But his training, except what Mr. Hambitzer gave him, was mostly gained by himself. He received the largest part of his education in the concert halls of New York.

His boyhood idols were Irving Berlin and Jerome Kern. He wrote his first song when he was fourteen. It was a tango without a name, and his first titled piece was *Since I found You*. Neither of them was published.

When he was fifteen, George went to all the concerts he could. He listened, as he said, "not only with my ears, but with my nerves, my mind, my heart." He be-

[214]

came saturated with music, soaking it up like a sponge. "Then," he added, "I went home and listened in memory. I sat down at the piano and repeated the *motifs*."

After Gershwin received his grammar-school diploma, he entered the High School of Commerce, but he wasn't interested. He had never liked to study, and he had not come to enjoy reading. After he grew up, Gershwin did study, but it was rather spasmodic. If he received an order to compose a form of music about which he knew nothing, then he would study hard in order to learn about it.

At sixteen, George entered on a job which held more drudgery than ever he would have had in school. But the fifteen dollars a week made him feel important and grown-up, and when he became a "plugger" in Remick's music-publishing firm, he felt that he was getting somewhere,—starting his climb, at least, up the jazzy path in Tin Pan Alley.

Reading the lives of the greatest composers, and discovering that in most cases their music, sounding new and strange to the people of their own times, was not appreciated for many years, you understand that great music becomes more endearing through familiarity. The more you hear it, the more you like it. When you know something well enough to hum it, or to whistle it, you are probably already in love with it. Many important compositions are hard to play, because of their technical difficulties or for reasons of interpretation, or because of great demands in the matter of instruments (if the composition is orchestral) and hence are not at first played very often. Today, with records and radio, we have more opportunities than our parents had to become familiar with new music. In the past there have been instances where a composer died before the time came when his works were known and loved.

This is not so hard to understand, seeing that even now the majority of people do not want to have to *think* about their enjoyments. They would rather go to a movie than to a museum, for instance, because in the first case they can be entertained without having to think. They can just relax, rest and enjoy. In a museum, the wonderful works of art or science that are assembled there make one think.

But it is really amusing to reflect that the fun music of ragtime and the popular songs had to be "plugged," that is—played over and over again, in order to be "familiarized." Now there are the radio, movie-music, or advertising companies to do this, but in Gershwin's boyhood days, it was up to the "plugger"—the music salesman himself.

Music publishers' offices in Tin Pan Alley were equipped (a word almost too elegant in describing such inelegant places) with "professional parlors"—also a gaudy, elaborate name for the tiny cells they were. These small rooms were just large enough to hold an overworked, dingy but upright piano. There were several rooms jumbled near together making up the "professional parlors," and in each room a piano. At each piano sat a plugger, playing endlessly all day long and day after day, the publications of the firm. It was Gershwin's job to know all the Remick publications and to plug them continuously. A plugger in the next room did the same, so that a din and racket kept up from morning to night. Actors and singers stepped in from Broadway in search of new songs for their acts. A comedian would need a funny song; a tenor might be looking for one with a heart-throb in it; a blonde searching for a new lovesong, or a little brunette dancer wanting a song with a dance in it. The song-selling plugger had to know them all.

Many of the vaudeville singers couldn't read a note, and frequently the plugger would have to play the same song over and over to the same customer, to get it into the ears of the singer, who would then go out and sing it to the public. It was a "racket" in both senses of the word.

But what an education! Many times a piece was written in a key too high or too low for the customer, and George became adept at transposing and playing in different keys on the instant. His hands were never still, for he played eight and ten hours a day. And that wasn't all. When evening came, the little army of pluggers was sent out into the cafés of New York to assist the song-and-dance artists who would themselves be plugging the new tunes into the ears of the public. George could improvise a dance routine until the notes slipped out of his sleeve by the hundreds.

[217]

It was an ideal way to study what the public liked. George began to notice that in the old publishing routine they had come to be afraid of trying out anything new. They were afraid that something too different might not pay. So they repeated the same old sentiments with the same old kinds of melodies to the same old harmonies. George looked around him and observed that the people who came to the cafés for an evening would have liked more snap and go in the music. In fact, the word "pep" was just coming into use. Gradually George became discontented in the "pluggers' prison." His own development in such surroundings had been to become self-reliant, alert to seize opportunities. It was no place to be sensitive and retiring, only the "hard-boiled" succeeded in Tin Pan Alley. He began to aim higher.

When George tried out some of his own tunes, they were at first refused by his employers. He kept them for the future. Unconsciously perhaps, this Gershwin plugger boy wanted to climb out of the coarse atmosphere of such surroundings into a clearer, more refined air. He developed a very important faculty— that of criticizing his own music. He threw away many of the songs he wrote, which he considered not good enough, before his first big success. He also developed a critical attitude for improving popular music.

Tune-writers made money; so did the men who wrote the words, though some of the tunesters were so untutored that they could play piano with one finger only, and some of the wordsters didn't even know what grammar was. Songs were frequently sprinkled with "ain'ts" and "gotta's" and other such offenders. But Gershwin was one who wanted to learn always something more—something beyond what he already knew. That was where he stood out in Tin Pan Alley. He had already learned to play the piano dexterously; no one-finger business for him!

He was attending a wedding in a hotel when the orchestra played Jerome Kern's *I'm Here and You're Here* and *They'll Never Believe Me*. The tuneful pieces won George completely. He rushed over to the leader to find out what they were. He made a point of studying all of Kern's songs, and trying to compose in the same vein. Then for a while Gershwin's music sounded like Kern. He was groping and growing.

Finally Gershwin succeeded in meeting his other idol, Irving Berlin, the song-writer. When he had heard *Alexander's Ragtime Band*, he recognized it for something akin to what he would like to do himself. He played some of his own compositions for Mr. Berlin, and was given words of encouragement which sent him away with his head in the air. He was also encouraged by the one-finger song-hit writer, Louis Muir, the author of *Waiting for the Robert E. Lee* and *Play that Barber Shop Chord*.

His experience as a song plugger changed Gershwin's ambition. Instead of continuing as a pianist, he would try to become a composer. After remaining for over two years at Remick's, he left. When he was eighteen, his first published song appeared with the title, *When You Want 'Em, You Can't Get 'Em, When You've Got 'Em, You Don't Want 'Em*. For all of that, Gershwin received just five dollars. The man who wrote the words received more than he did!

George became rehearsal pianist for a show, *Miss 1917*, the music to which had been written by Victor Herbert and Jerome Kern. After that, he applied for the position of pianist at a vaudeville theatre on 14th Street.

Here he had a most embarrassing experience. He was unfamiliar with the musical terms which appeared on the manuscript of some special music written for one of the acts, which was a vaudeville revue. At the first performance, after several other acts had passed off well, Gershwin started to play the opening chorus of the revue. But when the chorus girls began to sing, what was his amazement to find them singing something altogether different from the accompaniment he was playing. He supposed he had missed some cues. To make matters worse, just when he was feeling ashamed, imagining that friends or some of his family might be sitting in the audience, the comedian on the stage started to poke fun at the new pianist. He looked down and cried:

"Who told you you were a piano player? You ought to be banging the drums!"

For a time he went on a vaudeville tour as accom-

panist to a singer. When he returned, another opportunity came his way. Mr. Dreyfus, the head of the
Harms Music-Publishing House (the man who had once
"discovered" Jerome Kern), said to George:

"I feel that you have some good stuff in you. It'll
come out. It may take months, it may take a year, it
may take five years, but I'm convinced that the stuff is
there. I'll tell you what I'm willing to do: I'll gamble
on you. I'll give you thirty-five dollars a week, without any set duties. Just step in every morning, so to
speak, and say, Hello. The rest will follow."

That was a wonderful thing to happen to a boy
who was still in his 'teens, who wanted time to have
ideas and to write, who knew how to work and use his
time. And before long something happened which made
him famous—famous and wealthy overnight. He had
the pleasure of seeing his name on the billboards announcing a show with "Music by George Gershwin."
When the show, *La La Lucille*, was played in Boston
and New York, it was received with delight; but that
was not what brought him his sudden fame.

Gershwin wrote a song, *Swanee*, which was sung,
though no great stir had been created, when, a few
months later the blackface comedian, Al Jolson heard
it, liked it, and sang it in his show, *Sinbad*. Jolson had
been born in Russia and first acted in this country with
his own white face, but when he first blacked himself
with burnt cork, he became a "riot" as a "nigger minstrel" and funny man, and he acted with a black face

ever after. His singing of Gershwin's *Swanee* caught the public fancy, and the song spread like wildfire. It went to London, and was a rage there. Gershwin was made.

However, George was hankering after the idea of writing music for the piano. He had the imagination to know that there was always something in music of which he was completely ignorant, and he had the energy and desire to go after it and find out about it. Studying constantly even after his first successes, he had as many different teachers after he was grown up as he had had before. He kept himself ready to grasp any possible opportunities, and when the invitation came to write for piano, he was "on the job."

Songs were turned out one after the other. "Music by Gershwin" was becoming a habit in the show business. He wrote melodic, sentimental tunes, some of which did not become known until years after he had written them, as well as "hot," jazzy dance-songs, such as *I'll Build a Stairway to Paradise*. For this he received three thousand dollars, which was a big advance on the five dollars his first song had brought him a few short years before. It was near the end of World War I, when ragtime was turning into jazz; and Gershwin, being played more and more both in this country and in London, was giving the impression that he was something "different" in Tin Pan Alley.

The ordinary person who lacks a healthy curiosity and an inquiring mind will never be able to see or understand anything which is itself out of the ordinary. A gifted person who by his energies has improved his gifts and enlarged his vision is on the lookout for something new. These are the individuals who are helpful in pointing the way, and drawing the average person's attention not only to works of art and cultural advantages, but to the "something new" worth notice.

When George Gershwin was twenty-five, a gifted artist and fine singer, Eva Gauthier, presented a startling program to her audience in Aeolian Hall, one of New York's concert halls at that time, where the finest music could be heard. This artist had the daring to present samples from Tin Pan Alley on a program of classical music and songs of European modernists. It was like inviting Cinderella to the ball; and the questions were: How would she behave? and How would she be treated? Miss Gauthier sang a song of Irving Berlin's, one of Jerome Kern's and three of George Gershwin's. The announcement of this unique program drew a strange audience. The musical middle-class did not attend. The audience consisted of the highest and the lowest of music appreciators—the thinkers and the "musical slum."

Now Cinderella, as one recalls, behaved very well at the ball. She was sincere in her manners, and made no pretense of being what she was not. She danced as graciously as she knew how, and put her whole heart into her wonderful evening, so that the Prince was charmed by her genuine pleasure and appreciation, and she was invited again. It was the same when Miss Gauthier introduced the kitchen-music into the musical ball-room. The audience was delighted by the honest, sincere jazziness of the songs that were out purely for a good time. These fascinating rhythms were, as we shall see, invited again. The erstwhile humble little plugger in the Alley had been asked to accompany Miss Gauthier in the jazz songs, for who could rip off this kind of music with such a flair as he? From the dignified stage of the proper old music-hall came the strains of *Innocent Ingenue, Baby,* and *Do It Again.* It amused the sensibilities of some of the élite, and no doubt offended others, but it flattered the "musical slum."

About three months later, a concert was planned by Paul Whiteman, the King of Jazz. He wished to present his jazz band in the same music-hall to the great musicians and critics. He wanted to know their opinion, for he himself had faith in jazz. To him it was the new music. If Damrosch, Heifetz, Kreisler, Rachmaninoff, and the music critics would not come to the dingier courts of Tin Pan Alley, Whiteman would bring jazz to them. For this concert he desired a special dish—something composed especially for the occasion. Whom should he ask? From whom would he be likely to get the newest thing in jazz? He asked Gershwin.

George Gershwin refused. He was very busy now. Since Miss Gauthier's concert, George's time was taken up writing music for a show. He forgot all about Mr. Whiteman's request. Early in January he picked up a newspaper and read that he was working on a symphony. It was news to him; he wasn't working on any symphony. But it made him think of Mr. Whiteman's invitation, and it set him to wondering. Perhaps he had better not turn down the Whiteman offer. It might be a good opportunity. He could easily toss off a "short, regulation blues" for the event.

The more he thought, the more clearly an idea took shape. There had been a lot of talk about jazz. People had said it was very limited and could only be used in strict time for dance rhythms. Possibly he could write something that would show this wasn't true. Thus it was that he was able to say, later, "The rhapsody began as a purpose, not as a plan."

Gershwin was called to Boston for the opening of a show for which he had written the music. As he sat in the train he thought of the concert a month away for which he had not yet written a single note. He was pondering about it, aided by the steady hum of the wheels. Later, he explained:

"I frequently hear music in the very heart of noise. And there I suddenly heard—and even saw on paper—the complete construction of the rhapsody, from beginning to end. . . . I heard it as a vast sort of musical kaleidoscope of America—of our vast melting-pot, of our unduplicated national pep, of our blues, our metropolitan madness. By the time I reached Boston I had a definite *plot* of the piece, as distinguished from its actual substance."

The more he thought about it, the more Gershwin was pleased with his idea. He employed some dance rhythms, but since the piece was a rhapsody, it did not have to be in strict time or form, as if it were a minuet, waltz or rondo. He felt that he was going to prove his point.

The time was getting short. A large manuscript page of music cannot be dashed off in a few moments. As Gershwin finished his pages of the *Rhapsody in Blue* for two pianos, the arranger, Ferde Grofé, made the orchestral arrangement which was to be used at the concert. There was no time to write out all of the piano part, especially the cadenzas, but since George was to be the pianist that did not worry him. He simply indicated the numbers of bars for Mr. Whiteman, and left himself free to improvise at the performance. Such a feat proves that Gershwin had an excellent power of concentration. Perhaps his experience as a plugger, when he had had to learn to work and think amid a deafening din, helped him to develop it. It also shows that he felt perfectly at home at the keyboard.

Many people have no idea what it costs to give a concert. Piano pupils often think that all they need to do is to get up on the stage and play, and that they will receive all the money which the audience has paid for its tickets. Unfortunately, that is far from being the case. The artist of the occasion not only does the work, but he must pay the rent for the use of the hall, including fees for the ushers, pay for the lighting, pay for the printing of tickets and programs, and pay for the advertising. It all mounts up. The concert on which Mr. Whiteman pinned his faith cost him seven thousand dollars. The auditorium was packed, but he had given the best seats away, in order to be sure of having the people there whom he most wanted. This may sound like a failure. On the contrary, it was a huge success.

Before it took place, Mr. Whiteman had created an interest in his new experiment. He invited three music critics to a rehearsal. He explained to them that he was preparing to present a program of jazz music in the "home of classical music." He introduced a young man named Gershwin, who, he said, had written something especially for the jazz concert, and they would now play it. As the two walked towards the stage, two of the critics whispered to each other,

"Who's Gershwin? . . . Yes, who's Gershwin?"

The third, who knew something of what had been happening on Broadway, a few blocks distant, informed the others that Gershwin was the composer of some recent song-hits for musical revues and comedies. Their memories seem to have been rather short, for they must have known of the Gauthier recital three months before. This is an example of how important the plugging idea is. People quickly forget.

After the rhapsody was played for the critics, two of them were completely taken with it. The third didn't care for it, but admitted, in words inspired by the music, that it certainly had "zip and punch."

When the day came—the day for which Mr. Whiteman had planned so much—he had stage-fright. It was not because of leading his jazz band, but rather it was a sudden doubt as to the music he was presenting. He was afraid of the audience, and unused to playing in such an auditorium. He slipped around front to watch the people come in. Though they were arriving in droves through a heavy snowstorm, he was not encouraged. The aristocrats in the world of arts and letters were coming to hear his music-hall dance jazz! Was it quite the thing? He saw Victor Herbert pushing his way through the crowd.

Whiteman said afterwards that while they were playing the *Rhapsody in Blue:*

"Somewhere about the middle of the score I began crying. When I came to myself I was eleven pages along, and until this day I cannot tell you how I conducted that far. Afterwards, George, who was playing with us, told me he experienced the same sensation. He cried, too."

Everybody knows how the *Rhapsody* swept into popular acclaim with the suddenness of its own introductory clarinet *glissando.* If Gershwin wanted fame, he now had it. It was played all over America, and in England. He was invited again to England to write a musical comedy for the Londoners. For them, he wrote, as a compliment, music more in the vein of their favorite Sir Arthur Sullivan; music with a lilting gaiety.

Within two years Gershwin wrote music for four comedies, and he was invited by Dr. Walter Damrosch to compose a piece to be played by the Symphony Orchestra in Carnegie Hall. Gershwin lived in both musical worlds at once. At home in Tin Pan Alley, he was invited into the politer halls of serious music. Society asked him to its parties—and also made him work. But, he liked it. He never objected to being exploited by hostesses and pressed into enlivening dull parties by his playing, although his mother once told him not to play so much on these occasions. He explained that if he didn't play he didn't have a good time. He enjoyed his own playing as much as did his eager listeners.

When he contracted to write and play a jazz concerto for the Philharmonic Symphony Orchestra, he had no idea what a concerto was. He had even contracted to play his own concerto at seven concerts, and still he didn't know what a concerto was! He went out and bought a book on musical form so that he could find out what he was supposed to write. With this book at his elbow, on his piano, he set to work.

In some ways Gershwin makes one think of Puccini. They could both write in a room full of people. They were unperturbed by the talking and laughter and constant going and coming. There were times when George Gershwin used to mutter that what he needed was a little privacy, and then he rented a room in a hotel where he could be alone, and get away from his friends who were constantly at his heels. But when they found him and clustered about, he went on working just the same.

In another way Gershwin makes one think of Rimsky-Korsakoff. It was Korsakoff who never studied counterpoint and fugue until he had to teach those subjects. He had to study, then, to keep ahead of his pupils, so that he laughingly said that his pupils taught him. Even he sometimes wrote before he knew enough about his subject, as he afterwards admitted. He wrote textbooks on orchestration, harmony, counterpoint. It was not until after he had been appointed Inspector of Bands for the Navy Department, that he bought a set of wind instruments to study. Then he even wrote a book about the technique of wind instruments.

Gershwin's eagerness to learn kept pace with his new fields of endeavor. When he wrote his *Concerto*, not content to have it orchestrated by someone else, he began to study orchestration. He needed to know how to write for the instruments. At this time he studied with Ruben Goldmark. After the concerto was written, there was need of hearing it to see where it might be improved. In order to accomplish this, he hired an orchestra of sixty musicians, and in a theatre one afternoon, with a friend to conduct and himself at the piano, he judged his own work. He was able to make cuts and changes.

When the day came and Gershwin played for the

first time with a real symphony orchestra, Carnegie Hall was filled. Here was a jazz composer playing with an orchestra which contained not a single wailing saxophone. Three years afterward, when Gershwin was in Paris, he heard his *Rhapsody* and *Concerto* played in his honor. Wherever he went in the cafés of Europe his music was played back at him. While in Paris, Gershwin conceived another idea, and his orchestral piece, *An American in Paris*, was played in New York when he had reached the age of thirty. Among the "instruments" for this composition, he used taxi-horns! One of the themes was called the "sassiest orchestral theme of the century."

Next to come was Hollywood and opera. Gershwin was the only jazz writer who, so to speak, stuck his finger in every kind of musical pie. He was himself exceedingly happy in writing the music for his opera, *Porgy and Bess*. He loved his opera, and would play his music over and over with his eyes closed, completely enchanted by what he had done. He was thirty-seven when it was produced.

To this young man who, in his work, experienced one unique event after another, there were added two more accomplishments. He had the satisfaction of conducting an orchestra himself, and in the Lewisohn Stadium, over seventeen thousand people gathered to hear a whole evening devoted to his compositions. More than four thousand people were turned away on that occasion. The next day newspapers said, "George Gershwin achieved last night what only Beethoven and Wagner have been able to do"—he had "a program all to himself."

One wonders what more there could have been for Gershwin to achieve—the man who as a boy had turned up his nose at the "little Maggies," and who would not even go to hear the music one day at school. He had scrambled up the ladder so fast, that he attained the top with the opera. It was also the end, for not long after *Porgy and Bess* was written, he fell ill in Hollywood, and died there a few weeks later.

Someone has written that Gershwin "sang one song —a song of the city, the music-hall, the mechanical age." Stephen Foster had written songs of the heart, but they were old-fashioned when Gershwin came along and wrote music "reflecting the wisecracking superficialities" of a time when people were more interested in making "whoopee" than they were in their fundamental emotions. But the old-fashioned if good and true never goes out. Fashions change, but style remains.

His friends remember George Gershwin as being a gay entertainer, for he was happiest—when his friends were around—sitting at the piano, playing his music. Some of the pieces they liked the best were never even published. They were his own entertainment songs. One was about *Misha Yasha Tosha Sasha*, which he did for a party at the home of the violinist, Heifetz.

As if he had not had enough to do with his music,

Gershwin once studied drawing and painting. He became very much interested in art, visiting museums, and as he had made great sums of money, he took pleasure in buying fine paintings. A one-man show of his own paintings was once held in a New York art gallery.

Gershwin was athletic, loved golf, tennis and wrestling. When he was able to afford it, he had a gymnasium in his apartments. He hated card games; enjoyed backgammon. His most cherished souvenir was an autographed photograph from Prince George of England, who became the Duke of Kent. The autograph said "From George to George."

Unlike Stephen Foster, Gershwin did not write the words to his own songs. Tin Pan Alley always has its wordsters as well as its tunesters and arrangers. As time went on, his brother Ira, who as a boy had read dime-novels by the dozen, became the lyricist who supplied the words for many of George's songs. There were many shows that had "Music by George Gershwin" and "Words by Ira Gershwin." These brothers were very proud of each other and worked well together by the hour. As they were very different, each was constantly being amused and delighted by the other.

Gershwin never lost his heart to a lady but he did, once—to a dog. Whatever he was doing, even though he might be rushed to finish a composition on short order, he would always interrupt his work, if the little dog begged to be played with.

One quality which George Gershwin's friends felt

stood out in his character was his never-failing belief in himself. Whatever he attempted, he was sure he could do. Again one is reminded of Puccini, who advised: "Believe in yourself and work hard."

George Gershwin, born in Brooklyn, New York, September 26, 1898. Died in Hollywood, July 11, 1937.

IRVING BERLIN

"I found it out for myself."

A ship had docked in the Battery, the lower tip of Manhattan Island, on which the main part of New York City stands. Automobiles had not yet come into use, and the streets were paved with rough cobblestones. Over these cobblestones clattered a horse-drawn wagon, in which rode a family of newcomers to our shores. They were immigrants from Russia. There were six children, their father and mother, their bundles of clothing, bits of furniture, and kitchen utensils. After long days of tossing on a restless ocean, huddled in the hold of the ship, the children in the wagon must have been glad to be on land again. They peered out, looking with wide eyes upon the new scenes of the city streets which were to be their home. The youngest one of these was a little fellow of four named Israel Baline. He is the one whose story we are interested in, for he turned out to be a kind of Cinderella boy, who by his own hard work and cleverness grew "from rags to riches." He had been born on the outskirts of Siberia.

He was the youngest of eight children, but the oldest had stayed behind in Russia, and another was already married. Israel, called "Izzy," was small and slight, with large, dark-brown eyes, and black, curly hair. His father had been a rabbi, and when the Jews were persecuted the family fled—at first only from one village to another. But their flight did not come to an end until they had crossed the ocean to scratch out a living in the New York slums.

It was not long before the whole Baline family went out to help earn a living. The four girls did bead work. The middle son worked in a sweatshop. The rabbi father obtained irregular work as a certifier of kosher meat in a butcher store; and at the approach of Jewish holidays, he served as choir-master in the synagogue. Soon after the first earnings began to come in, the family moved out of their cellar into a tenement flat in Cherry Street. They were still in a tenement, but at least they were upstairs, where there was more air.

For two years Izzy Baline went to Public School No. 147. He was interested for a time in drawing, but singing came more naturally. He had a sweet, plaintive soprano voice, and his father—the erstwhile cantor —made him sing in Hebrew the words of the Jewish service. Many men in the cantor's family had been rabbis. They could all sing.

The elder Baline never lived to see what his son could really accomplish in music. He died when Izzy was eight, and the mother had to take on the responsibilities of the head of the family. As the youngest child, little Izzy could not be expected to contribute much to the family's support, at first; but he soon developed a guilty feeling because he was doing nothing to eke out their livelihood. In the bustle of the rapidly growing city, where each week brought new boatloads of immigrants from Europe, he soon began to scramble for odd pennies he could take home and drop in his mother's lap. The thought that every one else in the family was contributing more than he did, began to hurt.

One hot and sweltering summer day young Izzy decided to enter business for himself. He went some blocks away where he acquired an armload of *Evening Journals,* whereupon the city's army of dirty, barefoot newsboys was increased by one recruit.

The sounds of Izzy Baline's boyhood were a jumble of the noises of a great city—the murmur and splash of the river washing against the creaking, blackened piers; the foghorns and boat whistles of the waterfront, combined with the racket of huddling humanity like ants in a gigantic antheap without its silence; the roar of elevated trains; clatter of street-cars; shrieks of fire-engines; hubbub of street life with the jangle of hurdy-gurdies; cries of fruit vendors and push-cart peddlers; chants in the synagogue; squeals and whines of China-town, nearby; the rougher sounds in the Bowery saloons, which were punctuated in those days by the occasional crack of a revolver. These were the sounds Izzy Baline heard. In his blood was the plaintive wail of his self-pitying race, lamenting the persecution from which his father had fled—an old, old story to the Jews, who have been harassed and hunted since time began.

New York is not really an American city. It is a

world-city, made up of people from all nations and all races. In its lower East Side is the famous quarter called the Bowery, which includes Chinatown. In the streets bordering on the north is the Jewish section—the Ghetto. Jewish families are still living where they were when Izzy Baline was a boy, but they are different now. They are more tidied-up, more orderly, and the tough, rough flavor of the Bowery's earlier and more lawless days are gone. Who could have thought that the Bowery should be called in our day the nursery of American popular song?

In George Washington's time, more than a hundred years earlier, the Bowery had been a little village, outside the one of New York. Washington and his officers, no doubt, drank many a hot toddy at the Bull's Head Tavern, which originally stood on the site of the later Bowery Theatre. Farther uptown, as we call it today, there were farms and woods. Chinatown had not yet been built up.

The Baline children always had something to eat —their mother saw to that; but Izzy began to feel that he didn't help to earn it—at least, not enough of it. He sat on the tenement doorstep, hugging his skinny knees, and watched the endless stream of life in the streets— the constant passing to and fro of sad people, gay people, busy people, lazy people. All kinds—except rich people. There were none of them in that part of the city. If there had been any, they would have been saloon-keepers, or café proprietors, the kind who are rich one day and perhaps poor the next.

The boy on the doorstep was beginning to feel sick at his own sense of worthlessness. He wasn't any good to his family. He was a misfit. He had much better clear out. He would get out and live on his own—or starve trying. One evening after supper, without saying a word, Izzy Baline walked off and didn't come back.

In that neighborhood, in those days, such things happened all too frequently. Izzy Baline was only a boy of thirteen when he left home. His poor mother waited and watched for him. For weeks, if a neighbor's boy came to her saying that he thought he saw her son on a certain street, she would throw a shawl over her weary head at the end of a long day, trundle to that corner, peering at the passing throng, ever watching for her youngest. But always, it was the same story, she watched in vain.

Years passed before he came back to her. But he did return to his mother, finally—and when he did he was able to bring her presents and comfort, because he was rich—America was buying his songs. The old mother had not learned the new language, and she could never understand how her Izzy could write songs that America wanted. Nevertheless she was pleased, and all her former anxiety was forgiven with never a word of reproach.

You are wondering what the boy who was to become a song-writer did that very first evening when he

left his home. He needed a place to sleep, and he knew
where he could get a bed for ten cents. He went where
the hum of nightlife was greatest—toward the Bowery,
the Gay White Way of the lower East Side. It was
where all boys, who left home, went first to seek their
livelihood. There he sauntered into a cheerful saloon,
and began to sing a sentimental ballad, popular at the
time. It was called *The Mansion of Aching Hearts.*

In these days a wandering minstrel would hardly
be tossed a nickel or a penny for singing such a song,
unless we were enjoying it as the funny kind of thing
that people used to like. But then, people really cried
when such songs as these were sung, and through their
tears they thought them beautiful. It is an example of
ever changing fashion, which goes on in music as well
as in clothes. In a short time, the enterprising trouba-
dour had enough change to pay for his night's lodging.

He became a Bowery "busker," offering his singing in the saloons, dance and music halls—called
honkey-tonks, and such places where sailors and other
transients in town came to rest a while at a table, to eat
or drink, perhaps to dance and be diverted. Better
places of entertainment on this order were the cabarets
uptown. Nowadays we call these places night-clubs.
Whether singing the popular songs so much made Izzy
tired of the same old words, one cannot say, but he became very adept at making his own words to the tunes.
He studied the crowds, and came to know what made a
song "take." He learned what the crowd liked, and

[240]

this was one accomplishment by which he was later to make his fortune. But he didn't know that then! He sang, "passed the hat," and parodied the songs of the day.

When he was sixteen he was given a steady job. He became a singing waiter at Nigger Mike's, at 12 Pell Street in Chinatown.

It was really the Pelham Café, but everyone called it Nigger Mike's. Nigger Mike was a white man, a Russian Jew, who was given his nickname because he had a very dark complexion. His place was a rendezvous for people who went sight-seeing in Chinatown.

Once when a visiting Prince from Europe was visiting in New York, among the sights he was shown was that of how the other side of life disported itself at Nigger Mike's. This time it was Mike's turn to be thrilled, and he generously announced that the drinks were on the house. Before leaving, the Prince tried to press a generous tip into the hand of the waiter. But the waiter, somewhat bewildered, backed away nervously, having a hazy idea that if he were to accept the tip he would spoil his country's reputation for hospitality. The waiter was Izzy. The next day a reporter, Herbert Swope, astounded by the sight of a New York waiter refusing a tip, wrote up the story for his newspaper. That was the first time that Izzy Baline appeared in print. Years afterward, when Izzy had become the celebrated songwriter Irving Berlin, he sometimes saw in the restaurants of New York or London a face which he had once seen among the tourists at Nigger Mike's.

Customers drifted in and out all night long. Izzy soon acquired the habit of working at night and sleeping in the daytime. By early dawn, after the last of the customers had gone home, the waiters piled the chairs up on the table, swabbed the floors, and cleaned up for the next day and night. In the back room was a battered piano, and it was at these times, between night and day, that Izzy went back to the piano and picked out tunes with one finger—tunes which he had lately heard on the barrel-organs in Chinatown.

Mr. Berlin now says that he must have written his first song through being jealous; it certainly wasn't because he had a song inside him that had to come out. It was when he heard that a waiter and a pianist at another café around the corner had not only composed a song, but that it had been published uptown, that he and Nick—the pianist at Mike's—thought they would have a "go" at writing one. Izzy was to do the words; Nick to invent the tune. They worked and fussed over it. Sometimes the customers even threw things at them, tired of hearing their endless stabbing at this or that note, or trying one rhyme and changing it to another. But after a while it was finished. They called it *Marie from Sunny Italy*. Then came a blow. Neither of them knew how to write it down. What was to be done? It had to be on paper so they could show it to a publisher.

They went out and found Fiddler John, a Bowery shoe-cobbler. He played violin in the evenings. But he didn't know how music was written either. Finally they found a young violinist who did know, and the words and music were at last put on paper. The pair peddled the song uptown in Tin Pan Alley. It was accepted, published, and Izzy Baline made exactly thirty-three cents out of it. Nevertheless, it was a most important song to him, Mr. Berlin feels, since it brought him the most important thing of all—a real start.

But he wasn't Izzy Baline any longer. When his name was to appear on a piece of sheet music, he spelled Baline the way it sounded when the people of his neighborhood pronounced it; so it came to be Berlin. As to the first name, he didn't want Israel, it seemed too serious, and he couldn't have Izzy because that was such a silly sounding name. He would have liked to call himself Irving, but he was afraid they would laugh at him at Nigger Mike's. The piece was published with the names: "Words by I. Berlin. Music by M. Nicholson." He kept on making up words to songs, and sometimes at the piano he would try to pick out a tune for himself with one finger.

One morning after three years, he was fired. He had been left in charge of the café about six in the morning for the two hours when business was quiet. There was nothing to do but sweep the back room, draw beer for any early workmen who might drop in, and mind the cash drawer containing twenty-five dollars. Standing at the bar, with his head on his arm, he fell asleep. The next thing he knew, Nigger Mike was shaking his arm. He blinked, saw that the sun was already up, and heard Mike accusing him of stealing the twenty-five dollars which were no longer in the till. Mike told him to get out and never come back. He went. Later he heard that it was Mike himself who had removed the money from the drawer. It was Mike's way of teaching the boy not to fall asleep on the job.

He was nineteen now, and how he dreaded returning to the vagabond ways of sleeping in a Bowery lodging house! He walked further uptown, and again found a job as singing waiter. This was at Jimmy Kelly's on Union Square. He had gone as far north as Fourteenth Street. The people who came to Kelly's were a different type from Mike's customers in Chinatown. As it was in the theatre section, the clientele was mostly made up of professional entertainers—comedians, jugglers, song and dance artists of the vaudeville.

With the pianist at Kelly's, Berlin composed a few more songs. About that time, there was much excitement because an Italian marathon runner, named Dorando, was to run a race with an Indian runner, named Longboat. It took place in Madison Square Garden. The Indian won. Just then a comedian came to Berlin and asked him to write some verses—a ballad—which he could recite in Italian dialect between the acts at the vaudeville theatre nearby. Berlin had been delighted at the race watching the antics of barbers, bootblacks, and Italian fruit vendors who had come on the great day to place their hopes and spare cash on Dorando. It was about this that he made up a tale in rhyme, and then the comedian refused to pay him the ten dollars he had promised. So Berlin went uptown on Broadway —the Tin Pan Alley district—to see if he could sell it. In the office of a music-publishing firm, after the manager had listened to Berlin recite his piece, he asked for the music to it, telling him to go into a little room and the arranger would take down his tune!

There was nothing to do, but to go through with it. There sat the arranger with his pencil and music-paper, ready to write down music. What music? Berlin went through the words again, and managed to hum something as he went along. It turned out to be a new song, and he was paid twenty-five dollars. That was a lot better than thirty-three cents. Some of the songs, including *My Wife's Gone to the Country*, began to be hits.

It was not long before he became a lyric writer for this very firm. They were to pay him royalties on every copy sold, and to pay him twenty-five dollars a week while he thought up his rhymes. He was still nineteen, when he stopped being a singing waiter and entered Tin Pan Alley. After years of hardship and many discouragements he was at last to have a real chance.

Though he had never been in the country, having grown up in the streets and knowing only the hubbub of city life, it was Irving Berlin who wrote a rollicking song about

Oh, how I wish again
I was in Michigan,
    Down on the farm.

Stephen Foster never saw the Swanee River, either. To him it was just the two-syllabled word he needed, and on the map he found it to be a river in the South, which was also necessary to his song.

With never a music lesson in his life, and no piano of his own, but with a great desire to make up his own tunes, Irving would go to the office in the middle of the night when no one was around, and pick over the rattle-te-bang piano until morning. He finally learned, after a fashion, to use all ten fingers, but he never learned how to play in more than one key. It was easier for him to use the black keys, probably because he kept his fingers flat and never was shown how to curve them. So he has always played in the key of F sharp, G flat, however you choose to think of it. Later, when he acquired money and could afford anything his fancy wished, he had a piano made with a lever which, by pushing, would shift the keyboard, and mechanically give him another key.

In his new job he felt that he ought to write several songs in a day. For a time he turned out so many, that his publishers thought they should appear under other names, and they invented some. It has always been impossible for Berlin to keep a song to himself after he finishes writing it. He has to sing it to the first person he meets. He used to think it would be wonderful if he

[246]

could sing his own songs on Broadway. It wasn't many years before this dream came true, and he has appeared on the stage not only in New York but also in London.

Long before this time, he had returned home to his mother. She met him with open arms, and there were no reproaches for the run-away. It was, however, always a mystery to her that her little Izzy had become a song-writer. When he became very wealthy and bought her beautiful and expensive gifts, she was happy, but she never understood it. Of all the presents he got her, the one thing she cherished most was a rocking-chair, one of the first things he ever gave her. She would never part with it, even when he was able to get her something better and newer.

By the time he was twenty-three, he was happy. He was Irving Berlin at last. The boy who had run away from home at thirteen, wretched and miserable at heart, the boy who used to tramp the Bowery with empty pockets, peddling a tune to a publisher only to be laughed at, was now—ten years later—a song-writer of Tin Pan Alley, well-known in the theatres of Broadway. He had even been elected to a famous club of actors called The Friars.

By this time the pianists in the honkey-tonks had begun to push the melodies a little out of place, so that the rhythm sometimes had a hiccup, or sometimes hurried to fit in with the swaying and shoulder-shaking of the Negro dancers. This new rhythm was the ragtime which eventually sang and danced its way around the world as something new from America.

One day the Friars were going to have their big party which they have always called their Frolic. Their new member was asked to do his "stunt." He sang his new piece for them. With shoulders swaying, feet tapping, he sang and smiled his invitation to

> Come on and hear, come on and hear
> Alexander's Ragtime Band.

It was a hit. Everybody sang it. It spread around the earth. In time a million and a half copies were sold. Even more. There probably wasn't a home in the United States which contained a piano, in which did not echo the strains of *Alexander's Ragtime Band.*

Now Berlin was made. No need to worry any more. He could live in fine rooms; there need be no more looking for a corner of some fire-escape to sleep on. The Bowery days were past. The little street boy had become, in his twenties, the most popular song writer in the world. And he had done it all by himself. There had been no rich uncle to give him a boost. He had had no boost at all. He had climbed by himself over a road that was not only rough and hard, but dangerous.

His boyhood days, or rather, nights, spent in cabarets and music-halls had shown him the kind of music people liked for their entertainment. He was observant. He noticed things, and asked himself why certain tunes were popular. In this way he became so good at spotting a catchy tune, that he became, later, a music publisher too. He knew the kind of sentiment which would attract the crowd—whether the song was humorous or comic, a song of love, or one of yearning which brings tears.

He went to England, and ten years from the time he had been a singing-waiter at Nigger Mike's, he not only became a member of London's theatrical and musical circles, but was accepted by what was called "smart society." Early one morning about four, when he was in London, he started to compose a song, *The International Rag*. That very afternoon he was singing the new tune in the theatre.

Of all the compliments paid him, the one Berlin liked the most was by a boy who never knew about it. On his first trip to London his cab door was opened by a newsboy who probably thought he might gather in a chance penny. He never knew why the gentleman from America had lavishly handed him the English equivalent of five dollars. He had been whistling *Alexander's Ragtime Band*.

Mr. Berlin has never learned to read a note. His music is in his head. He knows it by ear. He makes up his tune to words he has invented, and dictates to an arranger who writes it down. He is wise in knowing what he can do, and what he cannot do. Therefore he has never been blown off his course as a composer, and remains a song-writer; but he has written more songs

[249]

and hits than anybody, not only on Broadway, but in the world.

No music teacher ever taught him the keys. He never knew that music could change from one key to another until he happened to modulate by himself one day. He said:

"I found it out for myself, and I was so pleased that I started working it in wherever I could, and I've made thousands of dollars out of it."

When he was in his twenties, he had what was probably one of the most wonderful moments in his life, and you can imagine that he has had many.

One evening, after sunset, he went in a taxicab to his mother's flat where she was still living in a tenement. He felt suddenly shy and timid, even with her, because of the big thing he was about to do. He whispered to her to bring his sisters and brother and "come for a ride." She held back protesting that she had to cook supper, and a taxicab ride was too expensive anyway, she couldn't think of such a thing. But he insisted so urgently that she followed him, and the family settled themselves in the cab. They were borne past blocks and blocks of busy streets, farther uptown. At last they stopped in front of a fine, new house agleam with lights. They entered and went through a beautiful entrance hall, through richly furnished rooms to a fine dining-room, where all was in readiness for dinner with a maid waiting to serve it.

Poor Izzy tried to make a speech. He had probably

planned what he was going to say, but he never said it. His feelings were so deep, the words caught in his throat. All he could do was to pull out the chair for his mother, let his family know that it was their new home, bought with a song, and murmur that his mother didn't have to cook supper *that* night, and rush out into the streets. With his cap jammed down, he wandered through the streets all night long until dawn, having had no supper himself, his heart too full of remembering the hard times when he had lived practically in the streets, keeping himself gay enough through it all to sing his way up the years.

The year after *Alexander's Ragtime Band* began to rag its way around the world, Irving Berlin fell in love and became engaged. He and the lady were both quite young; everything should have been ideal for their happiness. But on the honeymoon the bride was taken with a serious illness—from which she died some months later. Now the songs were sorry affairs—like their writer. He traveled around Europe to help over the bad time, still he could write no hits until one day, after his return, he left a song with his publisher which expressed his own unhappiness. It was *When I Lost You.* Instantly it proved a favorite. Besides selling a million copies, and bringing its author much money, it brought him something more important—a kind of release from his grief. After this he was able to return to the business of writing hit songs. Many years later, he married again.

A few years later the World War swept Berlin into army uniform. He had to leave his comfortable home where he had a cook, valet and chauffeur, and peel potatoes as a doughboy in Camp Upton at Yaphank. He wanted to go abroad and sing to the soldiers, entertaining them as some other actors and actresses did, but he was not permitted. However, a young man who had gone through the hardships he had as a boy, and who had been able to have wealth without becoming spoiled by it, was not going to let a little thing like that make him surly. When he heard that the General wished for several thousands of dollars in order to make the camp attractive for the soldiers and their guests, Irving Berlin wrote songs for a show called *Yip-Yip-Yaphank* which was produced in New York. Berlin's singing was one of the hits. This was the only time his mother was ever induced to go to a show to see her son perform. When he crouched on a great stage, all alone, dressed in khaki uniform bending over a pail, and sang about "poor little me" and the hardships of a soldier's life, he brought down the house. The show made eighty thousand dollars and the singing doughboy never took a cent.

Another song which made a hit from that show was *Oh, How I Hate to Get up in the Morning*. No wonder, for it appealed to every boy in any camp. They all hated to get up in the morning. But Berlin meant it more than most. Ever since his days at Nigger Mike's he had always worked at night, going to bed about dawn.

When he first saw *The Beggar's Opera*, he was entranced by it, and wanted to write show music himself. He and a friend in the show business, Sam Harris, built a theatre called the Music Box, a name he had cherished for a theatre for some time. He composed one musical revue after another for the Music Box, and always the songs kept coming. He never ran out. They're still coming, and if you go along the theatre district in New York, you can almost always see the announcement of some show which says "Music by Irving Berlin."

His songs have sold more than those of any other song-writer of all time. But it was hard work. Mr. Berlin explains his procedure by saying that after he has an idea, he thinks up a title. He considers the title to be extremely important. Then he works for the main musical idea, which he evolves together with the words. Sometimes he works on a song for weeks before anything is written down. His remarkable memory is not confined to music alone.

The song-writer has no hobbies; he says his work is his hobby. To his father he gives all the credit for his singing and song-writing abilities. He is a great admirer of the music of Jerome Kern. His first musical idol was the song-and-dance man, George M. Cohan. Nowadays, if one were to ask him which of all his own songs touches him most deeply, he would answer: *"God Bless America."*

The composer, John Alden Carpenter, once said, "I

am strongly inclined to believe that the musical historian of the year 2,000 will find the birthday of American music and that of Irving Berlin to have been the same." Jerome Kern said, "Irving Berlin has no place in American music, he *is* American music." It was Kern who was to have written the music for *Annie Get Your Gun*. But he died, and Rodgers and Hammerstein, of *Oklahoma* fame, asked Berlin to write the music. Berlin said he couldn't write that kind of music; it was "hillbilly stuff." Perhaps he had forgotten that the first things he ever did were the same sort of music. They talked one Friday, Rodgers left the book with Berlin and asked him to lunch on Monday, hoping that by that time he would have changed his mind. By Monday, Berlin had not only read the book, he had written "It's Wonderful," and part of "You Can't Get a Man with a Gun." Later, he was to consider this musical show his most professional work.

Berlin established a "God Bless America" Fund with the proceeds from royalties and royalty rights to this song, principally for the benefit of the Boy and Girl Scouts of America. Hundreds of thousands of dollars have been distributed. He wrote this "cause" song during World War I but, feeling that the mood of the public was not sympathetic, he did not publish it until 1938. He "timed" it perfectly.

Another proud moment was when the programs said, "Uncle Sam Presents" *This Is the Army*. Berlin conceived this musical show at the request of the Army Emergency Relief Fund, and the proceeds went to the

[254]

Fund. The song writer spent over three years with the show at home and abroad. Again he appeared on the stage in his 1917 doughboy uniform and himself sang a twenty-year-old hit from his *Yip Yip Yaphank*. Audiences were delighted and loved him. Rodgers and Hammerstein established an Irving Berlin scholarship at Julliard School of Music in 1948 to mark his 60th birthday and his 40th year as a writer of songs that his countrymen have always loved to sing.

Irving Berlin, born in Russia, May 11, 1888. Brought to America at the age of four. Living in New York, 1958.

ROY HARRIS

*"Our musical tastes are determined more by
ear-habits than by . . . discrimination."*

Toward the close of the last century, frontier life
in the United States began to come to an end. In less
than three hundred years our vast land had changed
from the red man's natural Eden of primeval forests
and prairies to a nation bustling with the complex activities of civilization. Just before the turn of the century,
during a last rush for land on what frontier was left, a
pioneer named Harris, accompanied by his wife,
reached Oklahoma in an oxcart. They settled near
Chandler, in Lincoln County. Besides the ox and cart,
the pair had a gun, an ax, some flour and sugar. With
the ax, they felled trees and cut the logs with which
to build a cabin. The gun was an aid in securing food.
They staked out a Government homestead claim, and
settled down for a few years to till their farm on the
Cimarron frontier.

During their first year, a son was born in the log
cabin. The parents—who had Scotch and Irish ante-
cedents—named him Roy. A log cabin seems about
as strange a birthplace for a composer as it does for a
President. Yet Roy Harris eventually became a composer, and he was born on Lincoln's Birthday.

[256]

In a few years, however the Harrises discovered that they would have to move elsewhere, since the climate was unfavorable to Roy's mother. When the lad was five years old, the pioneer father piled his little family and "belongings" on a wagon, and traveled to California, where Roy grew up. During that time, the country around him grew up, too. He saw a group of small settlements change into one big city; and the great grain fields were, in time, cut up into small farms. They became the orange groves and walnut orchards of the San Gabriel Valley.

Roy's mother, who could play the piano by ear, gave her son lessons when he was very small, so that by the time he was ten he was the star performer of the region and played in local entertainments. He went to public school where the boys who could not play music, ridiculed Roy's achievements because "music was sissyish." It is a common thing for ignorant people, whether young or old, to laugh at what they do not understand. When a boy's mother says one thing, and all the boys in school say the contrary, it is very likely that the boy will accept the opinion of the other boys. It usually takes a few years to find out that "mother was right." Anyway, the future composer gave up his music. He played baseball and tennis instead. He acquired a reputation for being a real "man" when he broke his nose, his left arm and the fourth finger of his right hand.

When there was no possibility any longer of his

being called a "sissy," during his first year in high school, he began to have lessons on the clarinet. In a short time he was playing in bands and being offered a position in a symphony orchestra. At eighteen, he started a farm of his own, where he grew berries and potatoes.

An unusual characteristic of this pioneer country-lad was his eagerness to study unusual subjects. He had an inquiring mind. Moreover, he was industrious enough to make investigations by himself. While he worked his farm he also studied Greek philosophy and continued to play the clarinet.

In World War I, Roy Harris served as a private. After a year, returning to California, he supported himself by driving a truck for the daily distribution of butter and eggs. Having by this time decided that he wanted to know more about music, he studied harmony at night, and attended evening classes at the Southern Branch of the University of California. He also read Hindu theology.

For a short time, Harris wrote music criticisms for the *Los Angeles Illustrated Daily News*, but gave it up to devote his time to composition. He said later that "a first-rate critical faculty is as rare as a first-rate creative talent and requires as much training."

When Alfred Hertz, conductor of the San Francisco Symphony Orchestra, saw a symphonic work which Roy Harris had written before he had even studied composition, he advised the "farmer" to stop everything else and become a composer. Mr. Harris was already over twenty when he decided to make music his profession. Happily he found the right teacher in Arthur Farwell, who taught him composition for two years, and who felt that in Harris he had a pupil who would one day challenge the world. With this teacher, Roy Harris made the most astonishing progress, for he composed a *Suite* for string quartet, and an *Andante* for orchestra which were selected to be played in New York at the Stadium Concerts of the New York Philharmonic Symphony Orchestra. The composer, then twenty-eight, "hitch-hiked" across the continent in order to hear his compositions played.

The new music of the Westerner won attention, and a generous patron helped Harris to go abroad for study. A year later, his *Concerto* for string quartet, piano and clarinet, was played in Paris, and was soon followed by his *Piano Sonata*. These compositions, showing a marked advance and improvement in his work, won him a Guggenheim Fellowship for two years. He studied with Nadia Boulanger, who has been the teacher of many of our present composers.

At the age of thirty-one, during his last year abroad, an accident sent Mr. Harris to the hospital for half a year with a fractured spine. European study was ended. He returned to his own country for an operation and during the long period of recovery, he composed a *String Quartet* lying flat on his back.

This was the first time he had ever composed away

from the piano. Always before, he had had to write while sitting at the keyboard. Now he was free to write wherever he pleased. When he was well, he could go to the woods with a knapsack, and in the silent forests, he could write down his music. Moreover, he said he could write ten times as quickly as before. His technique became more smooth, his style more contrapuntal and less harmonic. The composer felt that his accident had therefore advanced him ten years in his work artistically.

A writer on music and musicians * once wrote that the "melodic conduct" in the *Concerto* for string quartet, piano and clarinet, (which the composer had called more simply a *Sextet)*, reminded him of the awkward, staggering walk which was characteristic of cowboys. It was this concerto which, broadcasted a few years later, elicited many letters from enthusiastic music lovers of the radio audience. Harris, who has never been at a loss to advance his musical interests, showed his fan mail to the Columbia Phonograph Company with the suggestion that they make a record of his piece which seemed to be so highly appreciated. They decided to take a chance and were most agreeably surprised when the issue of records was completely sold out within three months.

Harris is the first American composer who was ever commissioned to write a work especially for re-

* Paul Rosenfeld: *An Hour with American Music.* J. B. Lippincott Company, 1929.

cording. When the R.C.A. Victor Company gave him the order, it was on the condition that no orchestra be allowed to play it until after the record had gone into circulation, though the composer was permitted to sell his score to Schirmer, the publishing house. The work thus called forth was the *American Overture*, the main theme of which is "When Johnny Comes Marching Home." Harris calls his *Overture*, "My Johnny." He explained that "this was one of my father's favorite tunes. He used to whistle it with jaunty bravado as we went to work on the farm in the morning and with sad pensiveness as we returned at dusk behind the slow weary plodding of the horses."

During five years, the composer was teacher of theory and composition in the Westminster Choir School in Princeton, and for the Choir he wrote a *Symphony for Voices*. The same Choir performed his *Song for Occupations*, which had been commissioned by the League of Composers.

Encouraged by the patronage of scholarships, awards and commissions, Harris has written constantly, mostly in large forms. Koussevitzky was eager to have the Boston Symphony Orchestra present Harris's *Third Symphony* in its première, for he said, "This is the first truly great symphonic work to be written in America." Toscanini, who has played very few compositions by Americans, conducted it in a performance by the (National Broadcasting) N.B.C. Orchestra and R.C.A. Victor recorded it. At the time, music critics said that "something of the crudeness and strength of pioneer America" had crept into this new symphony, and that it was "as completely outside European experience as the prairie morning itself." Harris has written a *Fourth Symphony* for Dorsey's jazz orchestra, a *Farewell to Pioneers,* a *Folk-Song Symphony* for chorus and orchestra, and many other works, besides music for the films.

A fifth symphony and a concerto for 'cello next took shape in his mind, though the composer's time could easily have been filled merely traveling about the country to hear his compositions played. It is an exceedingly rare experience for a composer, in his lifetime, to hear a festival period of two days devoted to his music. Yet the city of Detroit had a two-day Harris Festival, and his native Oklahoma held a Tri-State Band Contest where his tone-poem, *Cimarron,* was played.

The pianist, Johana Harris, the composer's wife, makes records of her husband's works for piano. The Harrises give joint recitals at which the composer lectures and his wife plays his illustrations. For a time they were both on the faculty of the Juilliard School of Music in New York, but since 1949 they have been teaching at George Peabody College for teachers in Nashville.

The tall, spare, raw-boned composer from Oklahoma has the appearance and speech that one would wish for in a Southwesterner. He has a streak of humor and a "gift of listening." Tennis and chess are his favorite games.

He has made a special study of medieval music,

and once remarked that "since Beethoven music has
been going downhill." He dislikes the music of Wagner, Berlioz, Liszt and Richard Strauss, but he believes
in a "new classicism in the future of music." The composer thinks that, "with the instruments which we have,
and with our present musical system, we are destined
to have one more great flowering of music, before we
are compelled to change our scale systems and our
instruments."

Mr. Harris has used themes developed from the
hymn tunes of the church life of early American society.
He feels that the music of the early Protestant church
has had a great influence even in our ballads and dance
music. Since he is himself the son of a pioneer, it is
interesting to read what he has written about pioneer
life:

"In pioneer days the social interests and activities
of frontier communities centered around the Church.
In the name of the Church people prayed and sang
together. Their praying and their singing was simple
and earnest. They prayed for rain when their crops
were burning up under relentless summer skies; and
gave thanks for food and shelter in the dead of silent
winters. And when they gathered together they came
from long distances; they came by horseback and in
sleighs. They were shy and awkward from long seclu-
sion, and singing released the pent-up hungers in their
hearts. The hymns they sang together were kept warm

in their memories as they worked the stubborn earth. It is not surprising then that the feelings of these early American Hymns have remained in the American blood, that the songs which we have accepted and popularized, such as *Old Black Joe, Swanee River, I've Been Workin' on the Railroad, There's a Long, Long Trail,* reflect these feelings, and that even today, festive groups often end up singing these tunes with choral harmonies."

Aaron Copland says that Roy Harris was born with a full-fledged style of his own. When we consider the music both Harris and Copland are writing, we feel again that the qualities which MacDowell anticipated in an American music are making their appearance.

Mr. Harris is very active in the musical life of Nashville, not only in teaching, but in radio work, writing articles on music for the papers, and trying to show people how to listen to his music. His Sixth Symphony was given its first performance in 1944. It has been said that his music always represents some idea, as for instance, his cycle representing in tone the growth of a people; and that his music is "eye music," conceived not for the achievement of beauty, but just cleverly contrived with intricacies, which can be appreciated only by a studious reading of the score by highly trained musicians. Hence it is difficult for the layman to appreciate or even listen to. This may be a natural result of his composing without a keyboard, though a Beethoven could write music of the greatest beauty long after he was stone deaf.

Roy Harris, born in Lincoln County, Oklahoma,
February 12, 1898.

AARON COPLAND

"To listen intently, to listen consciously, to listen with one's whole intelligence is the least we can do in the furtherance of an art that is one of the glories of mankind."

—AARON COPLAND: *What to Listen for in Music*

The Russian alphabet being different from the English one, it is sometimes difficult to transfer the exact sounds into our letters. When a Russian Jew once entered England and pronounced his name for the immigration officials, they spelled it Copland, though it was the same Russian name which is usually spelled Kaplan in English. By the beginning of the century, this same man and his wife were living in Brooklyn, New York, and their son, Aaron, who was to become a composer, was born there.

When Aaron Copland was born, George Gershwin and Roy Harris were two years old. Irving Berlin was twelve, and already selling newspapers and delivering messages, while acquiring a smattering of schooling. Jerome Kern and Deems Taylor were fifteen, and none of these boys knew then that they were going to become composers.

Aaron went to the public schools, and not until he was thirteen did he start piano lessons. Before long, however, he wanted to know how to make music, and the year after he graduated from the Boys' High School, he began to study harmony and counterpoint. He studied with Rubin Goldmark, the same teacher to whom Gershwin went for harmony and orchestration many years later. The year that Aaron Copland started his harmony lessons was the same year that jazz began to come in fashion.

Four years later he was among the first American music students to go to France to attend the American Conservatory at Fontainebleau. Afterwards he studied with Nadia Boulanger. Anyone going to France in those days to study music, was likely, sooner or later, to become a pupil of Nadia Boulanger. Not many years after this Roy Harris also studied with her.

When his studies in France began, Mr. Copland had already written a *scherzo humoristique* for piano, called *The Cat and the Mouse*, and this was played at Fontainebleau and published in France.

The young composer remained three years in France, and apparently made great progress, for by the end of that time he was considering an elaborate project. He had in mind nothing less than a *Symphony for Organ and Orchestra*. In the month of June, when he was twenty-four, Copland returned to America and took a summer job as pianist with a trio which entertained the guests at a hotel in Milford, Pennsylvania. But his duties playing with the trio hindered his writing. He was anxious to be at work on the Organ Symphony, more especially since his teacher, Mme. Boulanger, was coming to America, and, being an excellent organist, would play it on her programs. It was an opportunity not to be missed. The young composer gave up playing in the trio, in order to finish the Organ Symphony.

When Mme. Boulanger played it in Boston an amusing incident took place—amusing for the audience, not for the artists. The stage of Symphony Hall was filled by the Boston Symphony Orchestra seen against the background of a fine array of organ-pipes. Koussevitzky was conducting. Mme. Boulanger was at the organ console. The audience, having read in the program notes what it could find about the young composer—an American, too—was paying respectful attention to the new music. Suddenly, an unforgettable moment occurred. An organ tone would not let go. Instead, it billowed forth over the hall and seemed to grow louder with a horrible insistence, while the music passed on to other harmonies. Then everything stopped. Nobody played—except the tone. Mme. Boulanger gesticulated to Mr. Koussevitzky. What was to be done? Something must be done—and immediately. The tone was becoming unbearable. Something had gone wrong with the mechanism of the pipe, apparently. Mr. Koussevitzky remained, dignified, on the podium. Suddenly, Mme. Boulanger slid off the organ bench and disappeared from the stage. In a few moments the tone ceased, and the silence was suddenly as intense as the tone had been. Mme. Boulanger returned to the stage and took her place again at the organ. It was an occasion for applause. The Symphony was resumed. No one knows what was happening to the feelings of the composer during those moments, but after the Symphony came to an end, he received much acclaim.

It was not long before he received much more. He was the first composer to be awarded a Guggenheim Fellowship, which he held for two years. After that, various commissions for writing came to him, and he turned out compositions one after the other.

His music began to show the influence of jazz. A commission from the Women's University Glee Club brought forth two choral works, one of which is supposed to be Copland's first "conscious jazz." The summer of the same year, which was the summer after his return from Europe, Mr. Copland spent at the MacDowell Colony, Peterboro, New Hampshire. There he wrote a suite for small orchestra, called *Music for the Theatre,* which was commissioned by the League of Composers. This was soon followed by his *Jazz Concerto* for piano, first presented by the Boston Symphony Orchestra with the composer himself at the piano.

With these compositions, Copland began to receive more general recognition. Enthusiastic writers on musical affairs, said, "Here we have real Americana." One critic felt that Copland's use of jazz was "something like what Stravinsky did to the Russian folksong in *Noces,* Chopin to the mazurka, Bach to the gavottes and minuets of his day." He had elevated the jazz idiom to a high plane.

When the RCA Victor Company announced a twenty-five thousand dollar prize for a symphonic work, numerous American composers were encouraged to set to work. Aaron Copland composing his *Symphonic Ode,* found that he could not finish by the time set for the close of the competition. He submitted instead music which he had composed abroad, and this, arranged in a form which he called a *Dance Symphony,* won for him a fifth of the prize, the other four-fifths going to other American composers—Ernst Bloch, Louis Gruenberg, and Russell Bennett, the latter receiving two-fifths. But the *Symphonic Ode* was finished later, and played first by the Boston Symphony Orchestra. It had taken the composer two years at intervals, to write it. He had worked on it while he was in Germany, New Mexico, France, the MacDowell Colony, and New York City. He said that a two-measure phrase in his own *Nocturne* for piano and violin had been the "musical origin of the *Ode.*"

A visit to Mexico was the inspiration for *El Salón México.* Watching the dancers and hearing the players in a popular resort gave him impressions which he put into music to reflect the Mexico of the tourists. He took down no themes in a sketch-book, for he explained, "it wasn't the music I heard, but the spirit I felt there, which attracted me."

[269]

Feeling that if a composer could write music to appeal to young people, his own future would be more secure, Aaron Copland composed the music for an operetta for children, *The Second Hurricane*. It was written especially for school performances by singers from eight to nineteen years of age, and was successfully produced first in New York.

Aaron Copland is one composer who has given much time and energy to advancing the interests of his fellow-composers by trying to see that their music is played. A composer might write excellent music until he was blue in the face, but what good would it do him, if it were never played—if no ears ever listened to it? With another composer, Roger Sessions, Mr. Copland organized concerts presenting programs of new music in order that people might hear what was going on among makers of serious music.

Nowadays the highest number of listening ears are in the radio audience, and in the movie audiences. Mr. Copland's *El Salón México* was first heard over a broadcast by the NBC orchestra—the same orchestra which also broadcasted a first performance of the concert arrangement of the composer's earlier ballet music, *Billy, the Kid*. He has supplied the film music for *The City, Our Town*, and *Of Mice and Men*.

It seems as if the radio and film industries are at last providing our country's musicians with the patronage, the lack of which Victor Herbert (in common with musical historians) felt to be the real reason why our

[270]

musical growth has been so slow.

After Koussevitzky conducted the first performance of Aaron Copland's *Third Symphony* in 1946, he said, "There is no doubt about it—this is the greatest American symphony." Another American composer, Virgil Thomson, called it great music. This was rather a contrast to what took place when Koussevitzky first conducted Copland's *Jazz Concerto*. Many people in the Boston audience hissed. Some even accused the conductor of insulting them by asking them to listen to such sounds. Copland himself realizes well enough that new harmonies, or perhaps it is more correct to say new dissonances, sound strange to the unaccustomed ear. To him, they seem natural, and as the years go by audiences are gradually getting used to sounds that would probably have made Mozart tear his hair. For these new, discordant sounds have made their way into our popular, as well as our serious, music.

Mr. Copland received the Pulitzer Prize for his ballet music *Appalachian Spring*. His Children's Suite, *The Red Pony*, was the inspiration for a Hollywood film.

When he was a little boy, wanting lessons, his mother did not want to spend money for them because the four older children had done nothing with their music. For that reason, Aaron was thirteen before he could study music. Years later, however, his mother saw that her money had not been wasted on lessons for her youngest son.

Aaron Copland, born in Brooklyn, N. Y., November 14, 1900.

OTHER COMPOSERS

JOHN ALDEN CARPENTER

John Alden Carpenter, born in Park Ridge, Illinois, in 1876, was a business man who was called America's foremost composer, when his compositions were being played during the first thirty years of this century. This descendant of the first John Alden, who arrived at Plymouth on a November day in 1620, inherited a great love of music from his mother. It was she who gave him his early musical instruction. Before he began the study of composition, he tried to make his own music by what he called "painful improvisations."

While he was growing up and going to school, he had excellent teachers in music, and, upon entering Harvard College at seventeen, he signed up for all the music courses. There he studied composition with the composer and teacher, John Knowles Paine. After graduating with highest honors in music, he went home and entered his father's business. The George B. Carpenter Company was a firm which dealt in mill, railway, and ship supplies.

Though Mr. Carpenter attended successfully to the business, he was always composing and studying composition, too. He found time for both occupations. One time when he was visiting in Rome, he found to his delight that the English composer, Sir Edward Elgar, was also there. He had always been a great admirer of Elgar's music. He succeeded in persuading Elgar to give him lessons and advice, though Sir Edward did not consider himself a teacher. When Carpenter was thirty-two, he met Bernhard Ziehn, a teacher and writer on harmony and theory, and from him "learned more and received more inspiration than from all other previous sources."

Carptener had his first taste of success when his early works were brought to the attention of the music-publishing house of G. Schirmer through Kurt Schindler, the violoncellist, who was also a music-editor. Then his six songs, set to the *Gitanjali* poems of Rabindranath Tagore, a poet of India who was then making a deep impression, were published and sung with much acclaim. The next year, his first and one of his best orchestral compositions was played. Everyone was delighted with the humor of his *Adventures in a Perambulator*, program music which depicts in sound the sensations of a baby, while being wheeled around the city park by his nurse. Large compositions and more songs followed.

From Tin Pan Alley, jazz began to make its appearance and, though Carpenter was not a writer of ragtime, this energetic and truly American music made its impression upon him, as, indeed, it did upon all composers.

The conductor, Leopold Stokowski, invited Carpenter to compose a piece for the three-hundredth anniversary of the landing of the *Mayflower*, and in 1920 the

Philadelphia Symphony Orchestra presented *A Pilgrim Vision.*

Becoming interested in writing ballet music, Carpenter went to the funny-papers for a subject for his second ballet, and the result was the highly successful *Krazy Kat.* This ballet appeared at a time when many fine Russian dancers and artists had come to this country, having fled from the Bolshevist revolution of 1917. Diaghileff, a Russian producer of exquisite ballets, was highly impressed by "Krazy" as danced by Adolph Bolm. He thereupon asked the composer to write for him a ballet which would embody "the bustle and racket of American life" expressed in the terms of the fashionable popular music. The "bustle and racket" he had in mind were obviously New York, rather than America, and two years later Carpenter finished his ballet, *Skyscrapers,* which was produced both here and in Europe with much success.

Carpenter's music represented the "boundless energy of the Americans," which was the quality that Edward MacDowell anticipated in an American music. Carpenter said, "I am convinced that our contemporary music (please note that I avoid labelling it 'jazz') is by far the most spontaneous, the most personal, the most characteristic, and, by virtue of these qualities, the most important musical expression that America has achieved."

Mr. Carpenter died in 1951 at the age of seventy-five. His music is not now being played very frequently, but, in his time, it was important. All through musical history, one sees transition periods between the great flowerings of lasting styles. If compositions of these periods are finally laid on library shelves, it does not mean that they were unimportant, or did not contribute to the music of their time.

A few years before he died, Mr. Carpenter said, "American music is on its own feet now, and there are signs that it will no longer be influenced by foreign or refugee composers."

DEEMS TAYLOR

Mr. Taylor is another composer who has combined other activities with musical composition. A New Yorker, born and bred, he wrote the music for four comic operas while he was still in college and before he had had any lessons in harmony and composition. At that time he had had only a few piano lessons. He became a journalist and studied orchestration and composition by himself. His musical education consisted of ten months instruction in harmony and counterpoint, two years after he was out of college. Four years later, a symphonic poem, *The Siren Song*, brought him public recognition.

At a time when our native composers felt that their music was not given a chance to be heard because the conductors of our orchestras preferred to introduce foreign music rather than take a chance on new American works, Taylor succeeded in hearing his new works performed with great success. The orchestral conductors were not entirely to blame, because American audiences preferred imported music. This was partly because our musical inheritance was European, and partly because our faith in our own artistic endeavors was weak. Americans, for the first two centuries were primarily engaged in building a new country on a scale like nothing else on earth. It was natural that our people did not at first trust their own taste in such civilized matters as the arts, especially when we were being constantly reminded how young we were. But the twentieth century has seen an awakening. Americans know that our musicians, artists, and writers have much to give. The nineteenth century saw many American writers come into prominence. And there has been a rapid growth in this century in the importance of American musical artists.

Taylor's orchestral suite, *Through the Looking Glass*, became a repertoire piece for symphony orchestras, and was played in London and Paris. He wrote music also for the theatre, for films, and grand opera. When *The King's Henchman* was produced at the Metropolitan Opera House in New York in 1927, it was the most brilliant event of the season. Taylor wrote this opera at a time when Americans were beginning to be self-conscious about their own music, and people wanted an American opera. The Metropolitan's Board of Directors chose Taylor as the composer to supply the opera. The composer asked our lyric poet, the late Edna St.

Vincent Millay for an idea, and she supplied the libretto, based on a medieval legend.

Mr. Taylor has been editor of magazines, music critic for newspapers, radio commentator, and a translator of prose and poetry, as well as composer. He once said, "I think this country will produce some very bad composers and a few very great ones. Bad ones, because it is so easy to be popular here. You can please so many people by attaining a certain level—a level which requires very small gifts."

American taste in musical, artistic, and literary matters still has a long way to go for improvement.

WALTER PISTON

Walter Piston was born in Rockland, Maine, in 1894, and taken to Boston when he was eleven. He went through the schools there, and after high school, where he studied mechanical subjects, it was art and not music which attracted him most. He graduated at the Massachusetts Normal Art School in 1916, having specialized in drawing and painting. He had no formal music study during his boyhood, but he could play piano and violin well enough to earn his living playing in restaurants and dance halls. Then he began to study both instruments. During the first Great War he served in the Navy, and also played saxophone in the band. After the war, deciding that he wanted thorough music study, he entered Harvard and graduated in 1924 *summa cum laude* in music.

Receiving a fellowship, he went to Paris and continued his study of composition with Nadia Boulanger, whose name recurs so often as a teacher of our composers. He then returned to Cambridge, became a teacher at Harvard, and composed. In 1928, Koussevitzky presented Piston's *Symphonic Piece*. Chamber music and ballet music followed from his pen. His *Second Symphony* received the award of the Music Critics Circle. His *Third Symphony*, commissioned by the Koussevitzky Music Foundation was introduced in 1948 and won for him the Pulitzer Prize.

Mr. Piston has written valuable books on Harmony, Counterpoint, and Harmonic Analysis. He is highly regarded by musicians and has won a place of distinction among American composers. Though Aaron Copland once said that there was nothing specially American about Piston's music, seeing that his material was from European sources, his works have shown a knowledge of the kind of music which is so purely American, and that, of course, is jazz.

RICHARD RODGERS

Born in New York City in 1902, to a doctor father and a pianist mother, Richard Rodgers inherited a love of music and a gift which first began to show when he was a little tot of four. He could play by ear at that early age, and he invented little tunes which were genuinely musical, before he could even talk. His mother

gave him his first piano lessons, and he loved to improvise. He wrote his first song at fourteen.

The young song writer went to Columbia University
for two years. Then he and his friend, Lorenz Hart,
wrote the music and lyrics for a Columbia Varsity show.
The show was performed in the Grand Ballroom of the
Hotel Astor with great success. His college days ended,
Richard wrote songs and tried to sell them in Tin Pan
Alley, but he had only rejections.

He entered the Institute of Musical Art, and studied
under Frank Damrosch, H. E. Krehbiel, and George
Wedge, all well-known names in New York's musical
world in those days. He learned technique, harmony,
and—equally important—self-assurance. A gifted pupil, he was commissioned to write the music for one of
the Institute's annual productions. He also wrote a one-
act opera, a ballet score, a symphonic tone poem. He
knew in his heart that his music would not be for the
concert halls, but for Broadway's theatres. After three
years, he returned to popular music, and wrote amateur
shows with Hart, who did the lyrics.

Being asked to do a little revue for the purpose of
raising funds for the new Guild Theatre, he and Hart
wrote *Garrick Gaieties* for a single Sunday night's performance. They received no fee; they did it simply in
the hope of winning attention; and that is what they got.
It was so much liked, they had to repeat it the following
week. And again the next. Special matinées were
given, to which the critics were invited. When the critics

[279]

raved, there was a stampede to see *Garrick Gaieties*. It ran for a year and a half. It was their lucky strike.

Assignments now came in thick and fast—almost too fast. In 1926, Rodgers and Hart had three shows running on Broadway at the same time; the next year several in London. A Rodgers and Hart show was always a sure-fire hit. In 1930, Rodgers began to compose music for Hollywood. In 1943, the song-writer composed the music for *Oklahoma!* to lyrics written by Oscar Hammerstein II; since his friend Hart had passed away. This charming musical play won for its composer a special Pulitzer Prize, and also headed the list for long runs. There is, happily, always a show on Broadway with music by Richard Rodgers, and it is pure American.

SAMUEL BARBER

Another boy born to a doctor father and a pianist mother became a composer, though of a different kind of music. Samuel Barber was born in West Chester, Pennsylvania, in 1910. His aunt was Louise Homer, one of the great singers of her time, who sang at the Metropolitan Opera House with Caruso, Sembrich, Scotti and other world-renowned singers. When Samuel was six he began to study piano and at seven started to write music. At twelve he was a church organist, and at thirteen he entered Curtis Institute, pursuing the study of piano and voice as well as composition and the other special subjects a musician must know. After his graduation, his work won for him the much coveted Prix de

Rome in 1935, and he went abroad for further study. He received the Pulitzer Prize for his composition that year and also the next. It was the first time a musician had received it twice, and Barber was only in his mid-'twenties. His compositions include works for orchestra, piano, chamber music, ballet suites and songs. His *Symphony in One Movement* was the first American composition to be played at the Salzburg Festival before the war.

At thirty-two, the composer was called for service in the Army. While serving in the Army Air Forces at Fort Worth, Texas, Corporal Barber began to compose his *Second Symphony*. This work was dedicated to the Army Air Corps. When it was first played in 1944, it received excellent notices. Barber won more prizes, awards, and received other commissions to compose.

Mr. Barber likes to sing, likes to present his own works. He has sung in concert and radio. He conducted his own compositions in England, where his *Adagio for Strings* was most in demand. To his great surprise, he discovered that it was being used by a Paris radio station to introduce perfumes! At one time, being interested in the tonal possibilities of bells, Mr. Barber studied the carillon with Anton Brees at the Bird Sanctuary in Florida. He made his début as a lieder-singer in Vienna. He has also taught at the Curtis Institute. It was his happy fortune to receive, as a young man between twenty-two and thirty-two, more honors and more recognition from living masters than come to most composers during a whole lifetime.

In January 1958, Mr. Barber's opera *Vanessa* was first produced at the Metropolitan Opera House in New York.

WILLIAM SCHUMAN

Another boy born in 1910 also became a composer, though his path into music was altogether different. William Schuman, born in New York, did not have the musical background that Samuel Barber did. When he was eleven, and wanted to study the violin, it was because he wanted to play Beethoven's *Minuet in G* with the school orchestra. In high school, he organized a jazz band, and, though he knew no harmony, he tried to write popular songs. In his middle 'teens, he considered becoming a professional ball-player. But while in high school, he went to hear his first concert, and that experience changed everything. It showed him a world he had not known. Immediately he began going to all the concerts he could. While holding various small jobs, he made a point of studying harmony in his spare time. It was while he was studying counterpoint with Roy Harris, that he perceived where his path lay.

Schuman then entered Columbia University with the idea of becoming a teacher. In 1935, he went to Salzburg for the music festival, and received a scholarship in conducting at the Mozarteum. There he began to write his first symphony. Critical of his own writing, he withdrew several of his compositions, so that they would not be played until he improved them to his own satisfaction. When his *Third Symphony* was introduced by Koussevitzky in 1941, his fame began to mount in the musical world. Since then he has received many awards and prizes. In 1945, he was elected President of the Juilliard School of Music in New York.

REPRESENTATIVE RECORDS

This list of records is intended to suggest a sample of the music of each composer included in this book. It does not, of course, include all the music mentioned.

Most of the records listed in the 1941, 1953, and 1958 editions of this book are no longer available, and it is impossible to say how long the following list will be procurable. In all the arts, that which has the quickest burst of popularity is the earliest to fade away. In the two decades following Ethelbert Nevin's death, some of his pieces were to be found lying on almost every piano in the land. And in those days, before people could have music by the mere turn of a button, it was the proper thing for loving parents to give their children the opportunity of having music lessons, and the teacher came to the house. Every house contained a piano, if the parents could possibly afford to buy one. In the evenings, young people gathered around the piano to sing and make music.

Nowadays, when families crowd into smaller houses, the pianos have become smaller and most houses contain no piano at all. Instead, young people learn, in school, to play some of the band instruments. Therefore, with changing customs and changing tastes, the one-time fad becomes a thing of the past. Nevin's name is no longer listed in the record books. Neither is the name of W. C. Handy, though he died only four years ago. The so-called "popular" music gives way to newer styles more quickly than serious music. But Handy's "blues" had their place when Negro rhythms, melodies, and interpretations moved into American ragtime.

All records on this list appear in the *Long Playing Record Catalog*, Volume 13, No. 8, published by W. Schwann, Inc., Boston, Massachusetts. These catalogs, published monthly, may be consulted at any record store.

It is a pleasure to acknowledge the help of Miss Thelma Reichwagen of the Loomis Temple of Music, New Haven, in checking the list.

Records giving examples of early American music and the church psalmody of the Puritans are not available. At present writing, there is not a complete index of all the recorded music that may be found in the stores. Therefore if, for example, *My Days Have Been So Wondrous Free*, a song written by our first American composer, Francis Hopkinson, appears on any current-selling record, it is not listed in an index.

American Folk Music:
Sea Shanties.
Songs of the Sea. Norman Luboff Choir. Includes *Shenandoah, Rio Grande, Blow the Man Down, Lowlands, The Dark-Eyed Sailor*, and others. CL—948

Water Boy is on a record by Gordon MacRae, *In Concert*, which is mainly songs of American musical-comedy composers. Includes *Ol' Man River, Begin the Beguine, So in Love, Summertime* and others.
Stereo, ST—980; Cap. T—980

Cowboy Songs. Songs of the Pioneers. Includes *Sante Fe Trail, Last Round-up, Sweet Betsy from Pike, The Yellow Rose of Texas*. Vic. LPM—1130

[285]

Songs of the Cowboy. Sung by the Norman Luboff Choir. Includes *The Cowboy's Prayer, Last Round-up,* and others.   Col. CL—1187; Stereo CS—8278

Music of the American Indians of the Southwest.
Folk—4420

Gospel Hymns:

Gospel Hymns. Salvation Army. Includes *Just As I Am, Blessed Assurance, What a Friend We Have in Jesus, God Be With You 'Til We Meet Again.*
Lon. 5391

Billy Graham Crusade.   Vic. LPM—1406

Grace Gospel Singers.   Stereo. Ron.-lette 115

Negro Spirituals. Sung by the Graham Jackson Choir.
Stereo. West—15029

Negro Spirituals. Sung by the Tuskegee Institute Choir.   Stereo. West—18080

SAMUEL BARBER

Commando March. This record contains music by Walter Piston, William Schuman, and Robert Russell Bennett's *Suite of Old American Dances.*
Mer. 50079

IRVING BERLIN

Music of Irving Berlin. Kostelanetz and orchestra. Includes *Always, Top Hat, White Tie and Tails, This is the Army, God Bless America,* and others.
Col. CL—768

JOHN ALDEN CARPENTER

Adventures in a Perambulator. Eastman-Rochester Symphony Orchestra. Mer. 50136; Stereo: 90136

AARON COPLAND

Appalachian Spring, and the ballet suite *Billy the Kid*. Played by the Philadelphia Symphony Orchestra conducted by Ormandy. Col. ML—5157

STEPHEN COLLINS FOSTER

Songs of Stephen Foster. Sung by the Shaw Chorale Chorus. Vic. LM—2295; Stereo—LSC—2295

GEORGE GERSHWIN

An American in Paris and *Rhapsody in Blue.* Leonard Bernstein and the New York Philharmonic Orchestra. Col. ML—5413; Stereo MS—609

Porgy and Bess (excerpts). Original Cast. Dec. 9024; Stereo—79024

CHARLES GRIFFES

Pleasure Dome; Clouds; Bacchanale. On the reverse side is an arrangement of his piano piece, *The White Peacock.* Hanson conducting the Eastman-Rochester Symphony Orchestra. Mer.—50085

VICTOR HERBERT

Music of Victor Herbert. Played by Kostelanetz and orchestra. Includes *Ah! Sweet Mystery of Life,*

March of the Toys, When You're Away, I'm Falling in Love with Someone.　　　　Col. CL—765

CHARLES IVES

Three Places in New England, and *Symphony No. 3.* Hanson conducting the Eastman-Rochester Symphony Orchestra.　　　　Mer. 50149; Stereo—90149

JEROME KERN

Album of Jerome Kern. Paul Weston. Two records. Col. C2L—2; Stereo, CS—8049 & 8050

Kern's Music played by Kostelanetz and orchestra. Col. CL—776

EDWARD MACDOWELL

Woodland Sketches, Piano Sonata No. 4 "Keltic," Second Piano Concerto. American Arts orchestra with Marjorie Mitchell, pianist. Includes *To A Wild Rose, To a Water Lily.*　　　　Vanguard VRS—1011

WALTER PISTON

Incredible Flutist, a ballet suite. With Douglas Moore's *Pageant of P. T. Barnum* on reverse side. Hanson conducting the Eastman-Rochester Symphony Orchestra.　　　　Mer. 50206; Stereo 90206

RICHARD RODGERS

Music of Richard Rodgers. Kostelanetz and orchestra. Includes *My Heart Stood Still, It Might As Well Be Spring, If I Loved You,* and others.　　Col. CL—784

WILLIAM SCHUMAN

Symphony No. 6. With Piston's *Symphony No. 4*
on reverse side. Played by Philadelphia Symphony
Orchestra, Ormandy conducting.   Col. ML—4992

JOHN PHILIP SOUSA

Marches. Played by the Grenadier Guards Band.
Lon. LL—1229; Stereo—139

SUGGESTIONS FOR READING

OSCAR THOMPSON, *The International Cyclopedia of Music and Musicians.* Ed. by Nicolas Slonimsky. Dodd, Mead & Co., New York. 1946.

GEORGE PULLEN JACKSON, *White and Negro Spirituals;* their life span and kinship, tracing 200 years of song-making and singing among our country folk, with 116 songs as sung by both races. J. J. Augustin, Inc., New York. 1944.

JOHN TASKER HOWARD, *Our American Music. Three Hundred Years of it.* Thomas Y. Crowell Co., New York. 1946.

CLAIRE LEE PURDY, *He Heard America Sing.* A biography of Stephen Foster. Written for young people. Julian Messner, Inc., New York (1940), and Cadmus Books.

ABBE NILES, Article on *Jazz.* Encyclopedia Britannica.

CLAIRE M. REIS, *Composers in America.* The Macmillan Co., New York. 1947.

DAVID EWEN, *American Composers Today,* a biographical and critical guide. H. W. Wilson Co., New York. 1949.

DAVID EWEN, *The Book of Modern Composers,* A. A. Knopf, New York. 1950.

DAVID EWEN, *The Story of Irving Berlin,* Holt, New York. 1950.

DAVID EWEN, *The Story of George Gershwin,* Holt, New York. 1943.

DAVID EWEN, *Men of Popular Music,* Ziff-Davis Publishing Co., New York and Chicago. 1944.

RUDI BLESH, *Shining Trumpets,* a history of Jazz. A. A. Knopf, New York. 1946.

B. A. BOTKIN, *A Treasury of American Folklore.* Foreword by Carl Sandburg. Crown Publishers, New York. 1944.

BARRY ULANOV, *A History of Jazz in America*. Viking Press, New York. 1952.

SIGMUND SPAETH, *A History of Popular Music in America*. Random House, New York. 1948.

ROBERT GOFFIN, *Jazz—from the Congo to the Metropolitan*. Doubleday and Co., Inc. Garden City, New York. 1944.

W. C. HANDY, *Father of the Blues; An Autobiography*. Foreword by E. Abbe Niles. The Macmillan Company, New York, 1941.

ISAAC GOLDBERG, *Tin Pan Alley*. John Day Co., New York. 1930.

Treasury of Stephen Foster, historical notes by John Tasker Howard, foreword by Deems Taylor. Random House, New York. 1946.

HAROLD VINCENT MILLIGAN, *Best Loved Hymns and Prayers of the American People*. Garden City Publishing Co., New York. 1946.